Clean New World

The MIT Press  Cambridge, Massachusetts  London, England

Maud Lavin

Clean New World

Culture, Politics, and Graphic Design

Printed and bound in the United States of America.

Library of Congress Cataloging-in-Publication Data

Lavin, Maud.

Clean new world : culture, politics, and graphic design / Maud Lavin.

    p. cm.

  Includes bibliographical references and index.

  ISBN 0-262-12237-5 (hc. : alk. paper)

    1. Commercial art. 2. Graphic arts—Social aspects. 3. Graphic arts—Political aspects. I. Title.

Nc997 .L345 2001

741.6—dc21

00-056071

To Audrey and Carl Lavin

# Contents

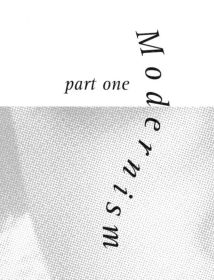

*part one*   M o d e r n i s m

*part two*   Post-World War II and Today

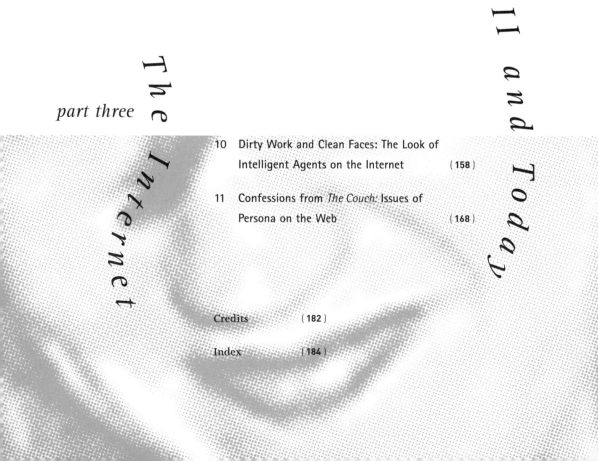

*part three*   The Internet

# Illustrations

**Illustrations**

# Acknowledgments

I am grateful to the National Endowment for the Arts for funding that made this book possible. I would like to thank friends, editors, and colleagues who generously contributed to the ideas in this book: Peter Beard, Jackie Brody, Jay Clarke, Ed Dimendberg, Johanna Drucker, Jim Elkins, Deborah Fausch, Hal Foster, Mickey Friedman, Barbara Heizer, Steve Heller, Pamela Ivinski, Karrie Jacobs, Jaron Lanier, Kim Larsen, Julie Lasky, Laura Letinsky, Ellen Lupton, Victor Margolin, Philomena Mariani, Annette Michelson, Lawrence Mirsky, Linda Nochlin, Chee Pearlman, Christopher Phillips, Mark Rakatansky, Michael Rock, Sol Sender, Michael Starenko, Sally Stein, Matthew Teitelbaum, Margarita Tupitsyn, Brian Wallis, and Peggy Weil. I'm particularly grateful to Anne Higonnet and Lorraine Wild for their creative, generous, and influential responses to the entire text. I want to express my thanks to Margaret Tedeschi, Kathleen Caruso, and designer Jean Wilcox at The MIT Press. And to Roger Conover, the book's editor at The MIT Press, my heartfelt thanks for his great insight, key encouragement, and gracious professionalism.

Parts of these chapters were given in lecture form, and I want to acknowledge the input of audiences and discussants at the following institutions: Cooper-Hewitt, National Design Museum; College Art Association; American Institute of Graphic Design design history conferences; University of Arizona at Tucson; University of Texas at Austin; University of Illinois at Chicago; Wellesley College; University of Maryland, Baltimore County; Walker Art Center; Vancouver Art Gallery. And my warm thanks also to my students at The School of the Art

Institute of Chicago, particularly the designers Glen Cummings, John Goe, Amy Johnson, and Grace Kendall.

*Clean New World* is dedicated with love and appreciation to my parents, Audrey and Carl Lavin. And finally I thank my husband Locke Bowman and my stepsons Kris and David Bowman, with love.

Clean New World

# Introduction

This book is about who gets to say what to whom. It's about who has the means to communicate, the power and money to get a message across, the passion and humor to speak, the openness and confidence to participate in dialogue rather than monologue. In aiming these questions at graphic design and the related areas of advertising, corporate identity programs, Web sites, and political photomontages and posters, I am looking in particular at cottage-industry images printed, broadcast, projected, or digitally transmitted in mass markets. I want to know what happens to private visions in public forums. For me and for others, graphic design is an umbrella field, defined broadly as mass visual communication and more fully as "an art form that depends for its efficacy on the degree to which words and images communicate a coherent message."[1] For the most part, it's a hard-working service field, a field that sees itself more occupied with translating speech into visual language than speaking. It is client- and product-oriented. Many of its corporate-client practitioners are instructed to provide order and clarity, to give their clients' companies the look, sheen, and promise of a clean new world. It's a fairly neurotic expectation, since designers can't really clean—they just cover, wrap, accent, or put into a clean envelope some messy realities. Typically, no in-depth communication exists in corporate design graphics. For me, graphic design fascinates, then, because it is a bizarre example of hamstrung power. In corporate service, design's most common function, it is implicated in both cultural stasis and change, but with only partial control.

1

A while ago in Minneapolis, I was on a panel with Ivan Chermayeff, a principal in the design firm of Chermayeff/Geismar. A star in the field, Chermayeff looked the part of the handsomely aging artist: tall, rangy, with longish hair and expensively understated clothes. Chermayeff was well known for, among other things, having redesigned Mobil's corporate graphics. His waves of clean gasoline sloshing inside the orange O were then seen by millions of people. But as we started to talk in the panel about how that image and its related identity program did and did not relate to what Mobil actually does as a corporation, Chermayeff grew uneasy. He didn't really know or didn't want to talk about what Mobil did. His task was to concentrate on the details of its look. Here was someone who had tremendous power to communicate visually and no power whatsoever to influence the content. And here was a field, graphic design, bent like most fields around self-justification, forced to talk formal visual issues and ignore its own impotency.

Because graphic design is so powerful and so warped (in most commercial practice) in its ability to communicate, it provides an exaggerated model for the same questions that dog other communication fields like photography, film, the Internet, and my own field, writing. Who really has a voice in our culture? Do we have public forums that are democratic, alive, open, fun, able to make a difference? Or are too many of our public spaces bought and closed off: the town square where speeches were protected by the First Amendment now deserted in favor of the shopping mall where private owners determine what is said in advertising spaces; the cacophony of public-access cable ceding to HBO; anything resembling porn on the Net potentially censored by schools and libraries; reporters, TV news anchors, graphic designers, and others hired to condense and deliver messages but to keep their own mouths shut.

Of course, like most people, graphic designers don't like keeping their mouths shut. For financial reasons, the same designers will often work on corporate graphics and on alternative, self-generated projects. So, this book is not only about communication questions, but also about the historical and contemporary track record of graphics in making powerful political statements, in functioning as intriguing personal creations, and in consciously influencing cultural norms. It looks back to the 1920s, to the outspoken designers who rode the first wave of mass media pervading the everyday—to Kurt Schwitters and the neue ring's Weimar designs, to Studio ringl + pit's ironic advertising images of women. It then moves to the history of U.S. corporate design and the positioning of designers like Will Golden, Paul Rand, and Sheila Levrant de Bretteville inside and outside corporate sponsorship. What do we do for money and what for love? What to pay the rent and what to make a difference? These urgent questions are filtered through design practices.

Some of these questions are answered by the ornery voices of people like Barbara Kruger and Stephen Kroninger, people who work with words, images, political and media references, anger, and humor. They can't be easily classified as artists, designers, or illustrators. Barbara Kruger refers to herself as an artist who works with images and words and not as a designer, but she is included in this book because she uses graphic design techniques, has influenced designers, and, most important, regularly uses mass-distribution systems for her visual editorializing. Stephen Kroninger has been variously described as a collagist, an illustrator, and a caricaturist; he, too, brings his personal voice into mass-media distribution. This role has been particularly difficult to achieve in recent decades when media monopolization has made it harder to get private voices publicly aired.

Nevertheless, it's a time when women have at last come to the fore of the graphic design field. Yet they still earn less than their male counterparts. Perhaps because of the continuing economic inequity with design firms, women designers who do self-generated as well as corporate work have turned increasingly to a mix of teaching and self-employment structures that combine to create semi-independent, multitasking practices. Such multitasking in turn has provided a persuasive model for the field as a whole. I offer a portfolio here of the work of some leading female designers who by and large work for institutional and corporate clients and in addition have a strong record of self-expressive work and/or public service—designers like Lorraine Wild, Rebeca Méndez, and Fo Wilson. Others like Peggy Weil, an interactive media artist, have used both images and words to question social and aesthetic effects of what public-distribution cultural systems and image makers do.

And what they do goes way beyond the limits of a given field. Our culture is dominated by the visual, so mass-distribution image makers influence what political issues we as a society discuss—why we talk about crime, for instance, and not overpopulation. In the chapter "A Baby and a Coat Hanger," I look at how imagery came to dominate the brochures and ads of both sides of the abortion issue and at how the rise of fetal imagery changed the abortion debate, in fact narrowed it dramatically, and I imagine how other images could broaden the discussion. In the section on the Internet, I examine how computer graphics influence whether we computer users feel controlled or in control, like plugged-in consumers or creative wanderers and discussants. These questions become most pointed in the case of intelligent agents, programs that monitor our use of the computer and then fetch research and do business transactions for us. Do they represent or repress our speech? The flowering of private thoughts and desires then can be controlled very close to home, even in our use of that increasingly common communication tool, the computer. Can we talk to ourselves uninterrupted? How can the relatively free play of design, words, and images on the Web lead to exploration of individual personae and community interaction? In the last chapter in this Internet section, which focuses on my participation in the cyberdrama *The Couch*, I unravel some received wisdom about these self-representation questions and assert a new, two-sided blueprint for forming personae on the Web.

Issues of the Internet return again to the main question of the book—the fate and look of private expressions in public forums. Can we express ourselves and talk to others with full displays of peacock feathers, unruly emotions, difficult politics, broad humor, keen elegance, information overload, and bad taste? Will graphic design contribute by revealing complexity or reducing for clarity, or both? Will communication remain kaleidoscopic? Or will all of this creative, transformative mess become increasingly filtered and clean?

**Introduction**

I see design—in its usual forms—as a hamstrung power in visual culture, but also a practice whose potential reach has remained largely unacknowledged by the critical field that set out to analyze it. Design history and criticism is a very young field; it has only existed as a regular presence in universities and art schools since the 1970s. Most writing on design has been preoccupied with analyzing design products, compiling designer biographies, and developing a historical narrative of style influences. There is, on the one hand, a desire to catalog basic information about design that itself is quite young as a pervasive practice, born as a largely unacknowledged technique in advertising in the nineteenth century, with a growth spurt and recognition as a profession in the 1920s, and not really burgeoning until its widespread corporate sponsorship after World War II. On the other hand, creating a style lexicon and a design canon also fits with the service mentality of how design is usually practiced: such writing is useful in the marketplace as resource material for designers.

I'm convinced, though, that writing about design needs to do more than this. So one contribution of this book is to approach design from the broader field of visual culture criticism and ask ambitious questions about power and communication. In writing about these issues, I aim to stir discussion, talk that does not merely react to the state of design as it is commonly practiced but instead is generative: encouraging designers to recognize and deal creatively with the cultural power they do, in fact, have.

My questions come at a particular point in the evolution of design history and also design practice. Design historians and critics have begun to open their writing to interdisciplinary approaches, thus acknowledging the multifaceted face of design and, not coincidentally, expanding its audience and discourse. Curator and designer Ellen Lupton did this with her 1993 Cooper-Hewitt exhibition *Mechanical Brides: Women and Machines from Home to Office*, where she brought together issues of product and graphic design with women's history.[2] There is a parallel. Recently for the designer, professional competition and technological diversity have encouraged a multitasking role. Typically, today's designer might provide a corporation with a visual identity, a mission statement, a Web site, a brochure, other advertising, and a trade exhibition presence—in short, a visual persona in the market. This diversity may still mean that the designer is curtailed in what he or she can say in a given corporate context, but it sets a pattern for a wide-ranging cultural involvement that the designer can pursue aggressively in his or her own work.

Today design sits at the intersection of cottage-industry cultural production, corporate sponsorship, and mass-distribution systems, such as magazines or the Internet, which are dominated by the visual. It papers our world, and its paper trail tells us much about how culture is funded and disseminated. It helps formulate our norms and even the speed with which those norms are constantly recast, much as corporate identities and publicly aired individual identities are now rapidly retooled. Yet, ironically, there is still much more writing about high art like painting or mass culture like TV than about design—even though it is design that operates as a kind of visual "fluid" connecting these other cultural products, selling them, and keeping them circulating, while also communicating its own messages.

We can't afford to ignore design's operations in a broader social and cultural context: design is a key marker in the historical shifts of institutions of funding, distribution, competitive reception, and audience. For instance, if writing about design were to be restricted to looking at styles, we would miss the important economic structural differences between, say, John Heartfield's monthly creations of covers for the popular photonewsweekly *AIZ* in Germany in the twenties and the design of explicitly political Web sites today. Looking through an economic lens, we see that today the mass print and broadcast media are monopolized and Web audiences are splintered. These two conditions together frustrate a broad participation in democratic discourse through the articulation of visual and verbal editorial voices.

I view my essays as part of a shift in current writing about design, one that connects design to overarching questions of visual culture. Conversely, those of us who write about design need to be careful not to repeat the traditional silences of the field, silences about the opportunities and also inhibitions of corporate sponsorship, about the changes in corporations and the marketplace (for instance, the current corporate pressure to rapidly adjust identities), about forms and forums that are open to cultural producers, about interactions with viewers who are also producers on the Web. Therefore, I've been exploring exactly these areas of power, economics, and audience in design and drawing connections to other cultural practices.

My own experience as a cultural critic and my thinking about issues of private cultural practice and mass-distribution systems has influenced my writing over time. So the early, historical chapters in this book were written when my writing was in a more distanced mode. These involve a dialogue between my own contemporary interests and scholarly research in the historically specific conditions of the 1920s. Then as I moved to writing more about contemporary issues, I began to develop a style that was more personal and that directly engaged the reader. I explored as well varied forums of distribution, writing for *Harper's Bazaar* and for the activist group Fairness and Accuracy in Reporting, for example, as well as Yale University Press. In these different venues, I also sounded out how different forms played in different forums as well as how different opportunities and curtailments existed with the different economics of each media situation. Broadly speaking, my role as a critic shifted from that of an observer writing in the third person to that of an observer-participant, particularly in the Internet essays, writing in the first person. Even in the earlier writings, I never pretended objectivity although I retained respect for historical research and context. In the more recent essays, I examine my own participation along with broader cultural developments. By adding this intimacy, I gained the challenge of writing about culture in a multilevel way and explored creative and varied forms of writing. As a writer for the cyberdrama *The Couch* for a year and a half, I was involved in the design of the site, working with designer David Steuer and the rest of the group, as well as with the evolution of its words and images.[3]

I've thought of my own writing process as building a multitasked critical practice, one sensitive to different audiences, morphing aesthetics, publishing economics, and evolving political debates. As a writer and cultural critic, I've published in a wide variety of venues, and my selection process of different forums has been motivated sometimes by love, sometimes by money, sometimes by both. My own span of cultural production—writing for large print-publishing companies like Hachette and small Internet servers like Cyborganic, the publisher of *The Couch*—mirrors the practices of many designers as well as other writers and other cultural producers today. So it is with the intensity of personal engagement as well as a sense of cultural timeliness and political necessity that I ask as a cultural critic about democratic, creative, personal, and profitable possibilities for speech in design and elsewhere. Using images and words, I want to explore who gets to say what to whom and how to expand the pleasure, democracy, and messiness of communication.

**Notes**

1. Mildred Friedman, *Graphic Design in America* (New York: Abrams, 1989), 9.
2. On the expansion of design history to a more interdisciplinary design studies, see Victor Margolin et al., special issue of *Design Issues* 11 (Spring 1995).
3. Peter Hall, "Log On Tomorrow . . . ," *Print Magazine* (May/June 1997), 52–57.

part one

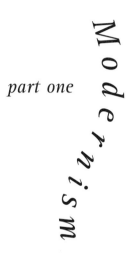

Modernism

# Heartfield in Context

John Heartfield (1891–1968), the German photomontagist known as an artist and a political propagandist for leftist, peace, and anti-Nazi causes, has been canonized only recently in the unofficial pantheon of modern artists. Although he was honored in the former East Germany during his lifetime, full recognition in Western Europe and the United States was slow to come during the Cold War years. Broad public discussion of Heartfield's Dada and later 1920s work was initiated by museum exhibitions: the 1977 Berlin *Tendenzen der Zwanziger Jahre* (Tendencies of the Twenties) and the 1978 *Dada and Surrealism Reviewed*, curated by Dawn Ades at the Hayward Gallery. Gradually, during the 1980s, Western art-world interest in Heartfield's Weimar photomontages increased because so many contemporary artists had turned to media-based work; Heartfield's leftist politics were made palatable by foregrounding his crucial anti-Nazi propaganda in publications and exhibitions. Then, in 1991, the Akademie der Künste zu Berlin together with two other German museums organized a major retrospective that traveled for four years to museums in Germany, England, Ireland, Scotland, and the United States, including the Museum of Modern Art in New York, accompanied by a massive, 342-page catalog published by Abrams. As impressively detailed as the catalog was, the museum installations, at least in New York and Los Angeles where I saw the exhibition, gave visitors almost no historical context for Heartfield's art, not even defining the figures lampooned in his political caricatures. The montages

2

were primarily shown as sanctified originals. Heartfield's art canonization, however, can be problematic when it threatens to upstage the history of the montagist's politics and mass-media involvement.

Though Heartfield himself showed his work on occasion in art contexts—initially, in the Berlin Dada exhibitions of 1919–20—he presented his photomontages mainly through newspapers, book jackets, and posters. He designed the photomontages to function within the contexts of photo layouts and news stories of which they were an integral part. Heartfield first began showing his work publicly through the independent Malik publishing house in 1916. Immediately after World War I, he also participated in the Berlin Dada group; from about 1918 to 1922 he was a cosignatory of the Dada manifestoes, a contributor to Dada periodicals, and an associate of Grosz, Richard Huelsenbeck, Hannah Höch, and Raoul Hausmann. The continuity between Heartfield's Malik work, his Dada production, and his later newspaper photomontages is his commitment to disseminating cultural and political criticism through periodicals and other formats.

So, rather than fetishizing Heartfield's individual iconic images, I want to focus here on the Malik publishing house in Berlin where he designed book jackets, layout, and typography from 1916 to 1932, and on the *Arbeiter Illustrierte Zeitung* (*AIZ*: Workers' Illustrated Newspaper), Berlin's popular communist newspaper to which he contributed covers and photomontages from 1929 to 1933. (Heartfield continued to work for both institutions from 1933 to 1938 when they operated in exile in Prague due to their opposition to the Nazis.)

To very different degrees, two smaller shows featuring Heartfield's work and organized before the 1991–94 blockbuster employed a contextual approach and are worth revisiting: a Peace Museum, Chicago exhibition of Heartfield's photomontages made for the newspaper *AIZ*, presented in both published and poster form, which was curated by Viktoria Hertling; and a show at Goethe House in New York of books, periodicals, and portfolios produced by the publishing house Malik Verlag, in which both Heartfield and Grosz were well represented. Organized by James Fraser and Steve Heller, this was the first exhibition of the Malik Verlag in the United States.[1]

Malik was an educational and propagandistic organization begun in 1916 by Heartfield, his brother Wieland Herzfelde, and their friend George Grosz. Heartfield, then a painter, and his poet brother turned away from traditional art practices and founded Malik in order to establish their pacifist stance against the war. Since government censorship disallowed founding new periodicals, Herzfelde took over the almost-defunct *Neue Jugend*, then a student periodical, and began to publish Grosz's satirical antiwar portfolios. In 1918, the November Revolution swept the Socialist Party into power with massive popular support, but leftist artists and intellectuals were alienated by its earlier support of the war as well as by its hiring of the right-wing vigilante *Freikorps* to bloodily suppress opponents. Herzfelde, Heartfield, and Grosz joined the German Communist Party (KPD) in late 1918; thereafter, the Malik publishing house served communist goals but was not an official organ of the party.

As Malik's graphic designer, Heartfield grabbed attention with his disruptive design for its periodicals and bold emblematic images for its book jackets. During his early Malik years, Dada aesthetics informed his work, as in his almost anarchic typography for *Neue Jugend*. Heartfield's book jackets were composed in a no less direct way, with posterlike montages of simple photographs and symbols—a design practice that reflected Herzfelde's policy of accessibility (a policy that even influenced the large typeface of Malik's book series).

*Neue Jugend* (1916–17), a pacifist literary periodical with an initial circulation of about 30,000, included contributions from Grosz, writer Else Lasker-Schueler, literary critic and activist Gustav Landauer, and others, and was the first of a series of proto-Dada and Dada political periodicals published by Malik. As each periodical was banned for its criticisms of the government, it would be replaced by another with a new name but essentially the same contributors. Unlike Dada movements in other cities, Berlin Dada was a politically engaged movement, and Heartfield and Grosz did not differentiate their Dada work from their Malik production.[2] As one of their contributions to the 1920 International Dada Fair, for example, they submitted the weekly issues of *Neue Jugend* from May and June 1917.

Two years after *Neue Jugend* was banned in 1919, Malik published an issue of 7,600 copies of an antimilitary Dadaist periodical entitled *Jedermann sein eigner Fussball* (Every Man His Own Soccer Ball). Heartfield's cover photomontage—of an array of Weimar government leaders, including General Hindenburg and President Ebert, as if posed for a beauty contest—is a satire of the layout of conservative periodicals; it is of historical importance as the first published political use of photomontage.[3] The issue also contained a Grosz drawing that was critical of the German Protestant church, an antimilitary article by Mynona and an antipatriotic poem by Walter Mehring. (Mynona—Salomon Freidlander—was primarily a fiction writer, and Mehring primarily a poet, in the Berlin Dada group). Anticipating the government's confiscation of the issue, the editorial staff marched on February 15, 1919, through Berlin neighborhoods accompanied by a frock-coated musical band. The entire issue sold out in a few hours.[4]

Other marketing strategies, though less sensational, were equally effective. Of primary importance to Herzfelde was to offer leftist material to workers at a low price while still producing books attractive enough to compete with mainstream publications. Malik sold Grosz portfolios in signed and unsigned editions, inviting the bourgeoisie, the target of Grosz's satire, to finance its dissemination to the working class.[5]

From 1920 to 1926 Herzfelde also published seven series of more populist books: "Little Revolutionary Library," "Collection of Revolutionary Works for the Stage," "Red Novel Series," "Below and Above," "The Fairy Tales of the Poor" (all children's books), "Science and Society," and the "Malik Library Series." This last included translations of Upton Sinclair and Maxim Gorky; a book of essays by Grosz and Herzfelde, *Art Is in Danger*, and a journalistic account by Fritz Slang [sic] of the 1905 sailor's uprising in Odessa, illustrated by stills from Eisenstein's *Potemkin*—a range designed to appeal to a wide audience. In 1922, introducing the "Kleine Revoltionäre Bibliothek" of eleven titles (including Zinoviev's biography of Lenin, theoretical tracts by Georg Lukács and Kurt Wittfogel, and Grosz's *Face of the Ruling Class* graphics portfolio), Herzfelde explained his rationale for producing such series:

This collection publishes documents, biographies, theoretical materials, all of which are designed to stimulate and develop revolutionary awareness and zeal. It should give the individual lacking time for extensive study the opportunity to increase his knowledge of the class struggle and to enlarge his revolutionary horizon.[6]

A 1923 Malik prospectus advertised four editions of Grosz's *Ecce Homo* ranging in price from 16 to 700 marks. The same ad announced paperback and hardcover editions of Lukács's *Political Essays* at 3.3 and 7 marks and four differently priced bindings of Sinclair's *Man nennt mich Zimmerman* (I Am Called Zimmerman). By 1927 Malik could attract 100,000 buyers of Sinclair's *Petroleum* and 120,000 of Domela's *Der Falsche Prinz* (The False Prince).

The principal designer of Malik book jackets, Heartfield created emblematic compositions and wrap-around images, as in the cover for Sinclair's 1924 *Der Sumpf* (translated as The Swamp apparently because The Jungle suggested a boy's book). Though some of his designs incorporated Grosz drawings, most relied on contemporary photographs—news photos, publicity images, staged photos—possibly to underline the topical relevance of the books; and most of the designs were black and white with red accents. Heartfield's cover for the 1924 Malik yearbook *Platz! dem Arbeiter* (Place of the Workers), a collection of political statements by Kurt Tucholsky, Rosa Luxemburg, Wittfogel, and others, consisted of four rows of news photographs of revolutionary scenes. In its imitation of newsreel film footage, this format suggested both contemporaneity and political activism, as did the Marxian headlinelike banners that appear above and below the photos: "Philosophers have always interpreted the world differently. What matters is to change it." And this: "The dominant ideas of an era are always the ideas of the dominant class."

Just as an understanding of Malik Verlag as a propaganda system is essential to a reading of Heartfield's Malik designs, so too I consider it crucial to see his photomontages for *AIZ*, a communist photonewspaper, in context. Though the Peace Museum exhibition I saw at SUNY Westbury was small—limited to some forty photomontages, most produced for *AIZ*, with a few additional posters and book jackets—it managed to relate the images well to contemporaneous political events. However, the show lacked any display of whole issues of *AIZ* or of a Heartfield montage in the context of its customary two-page spread. Unlike the Goethe House show, which focused on Malik as a disseminating institution, the installation at Westbury did not provide enough information about *AIZ*—or about Heartfield's role in selling the newspaper.

*AIZ* was in existence, in one form or another, from 1921 to 1938, and was issued weekly after 1926. Although not the official press of the party, it was the leading communist newspaper in the Weimar socialist republic, an era when disillusionment with the corrupt judicial system and police brutality of the Weimar government as well as enthusiasm for the Soviet revolution caused the German Communist Party to function as a viable minority party in Germany. However, *AIZ* differed from the Russian party line in its vehement, active opposition to the Nazis when they began to rise in power in the late twenties.

*AIZ*'s contents and coverage were aimed at the working class (a 1929 self-administered survey showed that its readership consisted of 42 percent skilled laborers and 33 percent unskilled). Heartfield produced photomontages for *AIZ* at roughly a monthly rate beginning in 1929. During that time the paper's circulation grew from 350,000 to 500,000 readers in 1931. Even at its peak, most readers bought copies on the newsstand, so there was great pressure on the cover image to sell the paper. This is one reason why many of Heartfield's *AIZ* covers—such as *The meaning of the Hitler salute. Motto: Millions stand behind me!* (Oct. 16, 1932), the famous photomontage of a saluting Hitler being paid off by a colossal figure of a capitalist—have a direct, posterlike character (fig. 2.1).

Heartfield's post-1924 "contemporary history photomontages" (as he termed them) were most often based on photojournalism taken from his own archive, one built from newspaper clippings and material found at picture agencies. At other times, Heartfield staged his own photographs but remained within photojournalistic formats.

To open up an issue of *AIZ* is to realize how embedded the meaning of Heartfield's work is in its mass-media framework. For example, *Adolf, the superman: Swallows gold and spouts junk* (July 17, 1932), another well-known image that superimposes a news photo of Hitler speaking at a rally with photos of a skeletal rib cage, a belt, a pile of coins, and a swastika, does indeed, as the exhibition notes, "portray Hitler as the spokesman of German capitalism." But it is precisely this alliance that is spelled out in the narrative, photographic layout of the newspaper as a whole. The cover of the July 17, 1932, *AIZ* presents two half-page portraits of men: one in a Nazi uniform is identified as the wealthy Prince August Wilhelm of Prussia; the other, an unknown worker named Paul Michel whose leg was lost in an accident, is labeled "A civilian cripple since 1910." The reader is told that this worker's welfare payments were reduced by Nazi legislation, and the headline asks if two members of such different social classes can support the same Nazi regime: "Prince and worker in one party?" (fig. 2.2a,b,c).

On page one of the same issue runs a half-page news photo of a workers' demonstration in Detroit being brutally dispersed by police, with a caption that alludes to the contradiction posed by the cover image: "Never can the party of princes and millionaires interest the workers." Nazism is here aligned textually with capitalism and police brutality to workers. The connection is pushed further; below the photograph of the demonstration are three smaller photos documenting confrontations between Nazi members and workers. Opposite this is the full-page Heartfield photomontage of Hitler "swallowing gold and spouting junk."

Though famous as an independent iconic image, this photomontage depends on its position within the photojournalistic narrative fully to convey its import—that Hitler and the Nazis are fed by specifically capitalist funding. (In the same issue is a story on the financiers such as Fritz Thyssen who, according to *AIZ*'s claim, contributed to Hitler.) In its similarities to the straight photograph of a "news event," the Heartfield photomontage assumes a documentary truth-value; yet in its differences, it suggests a political reality that is obscured by conventional media representations and party rhetoric. The Heartfield image thus exists in a dialogue with the photojournalism that surrounds it, raising questions of verism, manipulation, and belief.

Heartfield's contribution to political photomontage—some would say his creation of that practice—is that his images direct a rereading of

John Heartfield, *The meaning of the Hitler salute. Motto: Millions stand behind me! A little man asks for large gifts,* *Arbeiter Illustrierte Zeitung* XI, no. 42 (Oct. 16, 1932). Courtesy of the General Research Division, The New York Public Library, Astor, Lenox and Tilden Foundations.
(2.1)

**Heartfield in Context**

commercial mass media as well as function as strong political polemics.[7]
A good example of this critique is Heartfield's photograph of a head
swathed in newspapers, *Those who read bourgeois newspapers will become blind and
deaf* (Feb. 9, 1930), which *AIZ* used to illustrate a story on the deceptive
practices of the Catholic and bourgeois press. Page one shows two almost
identical photographs—one straight, the other retouched—of a German
woman painter, Keimer-Dinkelbuehler, sitting in front of her easel at the
Vatican where she has been commissioned to paint the Pope's portrait. In
the manipulated image, the *AIZ* caption explains, her skirt has been
lengthened by the bourgeois press to cover her legs. The suggestion is
that if such an image is falsified, no photograph, no truth, is safe from
manipulation. Opposite the two photos, on page two, is the full-page
Heartfield photograph of the anonymous head smothered in newspapers.
The newspapers are mainstream socialist ones; the object of Heartfield's
ridicule is the opposition and its manipulation of reality. Though it

retains a degree of photographic verism, Heartfield's photograph is obviously staged. Here, then, he uses artifice to expose the falsely "true" appearances of conventional photojournalism (fig. 2.3a,b).

At times, Heartfield goes to great lengths to remind his viewers that his photomontages are mostly constructed of bits of unaltered photojournalism. In *Goering: The executioner of the Third Reich* (*AIZ*, Sept. 14, 1933), Heartfield identifies Nazi minister Hermann Goering with the Reichstag fire, an act of arson that the Nazis laid on a communist conspiracy and used as an excuse to outlaw the party and jail its leaders. In the photomontage, Goering, wearing a bloodied Nazi uniform and holding an ax, looms in the foreground, with the burning Reichstag in the background. His face is contorted in an expression between a bellow and a snarl, and the accompanying text, which labels Goering as the real arsonist, concludes: "Photomontage by John Heartfield. The face of Goering is taken from an original photograph and was not retouched." In effect, this

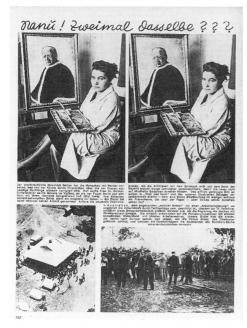

First and second pages, *Arbeiter Illustrierte Zeitung* IX, 6 (Feb. 9, 1930), photomontage by John Heartfield. First page demonstrates retouching of photographs by bourgeois press: "Well! Twice the same???" Page two: "Those who read bourgeois newspapers will become blind and deaf. Away with these debilitating bandages." Courtesy of the Staatsbibliothek zu Berlin Preussischer Kulturbesitz.

(2.3 a,b)

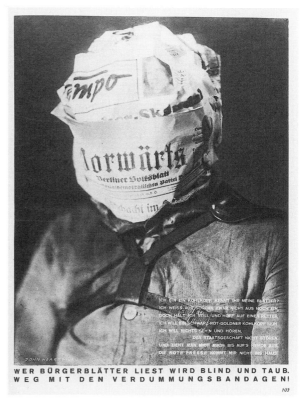

John Heartfield, *Goering: The executioner of the Third Reich,*
*Arbeiter Illustrierte Zeitung* XII, no. 36 (Sept. 14, 1933). At bottom: "Special Number: Reichstag's inflammatory law proce-
dures/counter procedures." Courtesy of the General Research
Division, The New York Public Library, Astor, Lenox and Tilden
Foundations.
**(2.4)**

is a directive to read the photographic fragments as indexical, bearing a one-to-one relationship with reality (fig. 2.4).

Heartfield's brother Wieland often collaborated with him on the written text, and they frequently used direct statements from the mass media—or ones that sounded as if they were quotations. For example, in *Hurrah Die Butter ist all!* (Hurrah, the butter is gone!) (*AIZ*, Dec. 19, 1935), Heartfield constructed an image of a family happily complying with the government slogan "Guns Instead of Butter" by eating iron. Under the caption is added this Goering statement justifying the government's rearmament program during a decline in the nation's standard of living: "Iron has always made a country strong; butter and lard have at most made the people fat." The quote, from a speech given by Goering in Hamburg, is typical of a media excerpt appropriated and/or adapted by the Herzfelde brothers to expose the cruel reality under the rhetoric.

In fragmenting and recomposing media excerpts, Heartfield commented on media constructions of reality—a critique that began during his Dada period and continued afterward. Heartfield invoked the verism connoted by photojournalistic fragments in creating his illusions, and thus his photomontages imply a more "truly" seen event; they seem to reveal the absurdities inherent in the real. Visually, this can amount to exposing the unseen aspects of a situation as in the montaged X-ray view of Hitler swallowing capitalist gold. What is significant is that the illusionism of Heartfield's *AIZ* work both depends on and refutes the so-called truth of photojournalism. Further, the meaning of Heartfield's *AIZ* pages is determined by the text and images that accompany them, and in a larger sense, by the ideology of *AIZ* as a disseminating institution.

Such a contextual reading continues to be urgent today in considering Heartfield's impact on contemporary artists—like Krzysztof Wodiczko with his locally based, largely art-world-advertised installations and Stephen Kroninger with his montage caricatures for mass-market magazines and newspapers—and a reminder that there exists more than a formal and political kinship. For these contemporary artists, too, their distribution and marketing systems powerfully mediate their work's reception.

**Notes**

1. *John Heartfield Photomontages 1919–1959* was curated by Viktoria Hertling for The Peace Museum, Chicago, and the Malik Verlag exhibition by James Fraser and Steve Heller. A catalog was published for the Malik exhibition, *The Malik Verlag 1916–1947* (New York: Goethe House, 1984).

2. In a general sense, all Dada art can be considered political in that it addresses issues of language and representation. Berlin Dada, however, was the one Dada group overtly involved in political struggle, specifically societal events during and after the Weimar revolution.

3. Dawn Ades, *Photomontage* (New York: Pantheon, 1976), 11.

4. On the basis of this *Jedermann* issue, charges were brought against Herzfelde as the editor and Mehring as a writer for "seeking to bring the Reichswehr into contempt and distributing indecent publications." Although neither was jailed at the time, Herzfelde was later imprisoned without a hearing from March 7 to March 20, 1919, along with many other communists following a general strike in Berlin. Malik's history is marked by a series of major censorship trials instigated by the Weimar government, the most well known being George Grosz's 1928–30 trial for blasphemy. This case centered around Malik's publication of Grosz's drawing depicting Christ in a gas mask. Called *Shut Up and Do Your Duty*, the drawing protested the fate of men forced into the military, particularly those of the soldiers who had been drafted and died in World War I. The case went through several trials and retrials, creating judicial, theological, and even legislative controversies. In the end, Grosz and Herzfelde as his publisher were acquitted, but the drawings were confiscated and printing blocks destroyed, reflecting the confused state of justice in the Weimar Republic. See Beth Irwin Lewis, *George Grosz: Art and Politics in the Weimar Republic* (Madison: University of Wisconsin Press, 1971), 70–71, 74, 221–225.

5. Grosz portfolios of prints and/or drawings published by Malik include: *Kleine Grosz-Mappe* (Small Grosz Portfolio), 1917; *Erste Grosz-Mappe*, 1917; *Gott mit uns*, 1920; *Ecce Homo*, 1923; and *Hintergrund* (Background), 1928.

6. Wieland Herzfelde as quoted in *The Malik Verlag, 1916–1947* (New York: Goethe House, 1984), 36.

7. This involvement of the viewer in decoding mass-media images recalls Walter Benjamin's admiration for Heartfield in his 1934 essay "The Author as Producer," in which Benjamin calls for a particular kind of political art: "The best political tendency is wrong if it does not demonstrate the attitude with which it is to be followed. . . . What matters, therefore, is the exemplary character of production, which is able first to induce other producers to produce, and second to put an improved apparatus at their disposal. And this apparatus is better the more consumers it is able to turn into producers—that is readers or spectators into collaborators" (Walter Benjamin, "The Author as Producer," in *Reflections*, ed. Peter Demetz, trans. Edmund Jephcott (New York: Harcourt Brace Jovanovich, 1978), 233).

**Heartfield in Context**

# For Love, Modernism, or Money:

## Kurt Schwitters and the Circle of
## New Advertising Designers

In 1990, the year when the much-heralded reunification of Germany had finally taken place, German celebrations of unity were overshadowed almost immediately by anxiety about its cost. Unemployment in the East and financial drain in the West became unification's reality test. The tensions between the dream and the reality of one Germany stirred debates about the country's public policies. Previously, in the helter-skelter rush to unification in the East, those urging an embrace of capitalism had temporarily silenced those whose voices were bent on preserving the tightly woven safety net of social services that were established under communism. Now the silence had been broken, and at issue once more was the uneasy mix of hard-core capitalism and German democratic socialism. Heated debates erupted about such social services as day care, unemployment benefits, and health care—particularly the right to abortion.

Germany's political debates about economic and social issues then and in the unification years immediately following were strangely reminiscent of tensions during the Weimar Republic, the only other time in Germany's history when the country was unified and democratic. During the Weimar years (1918–33), Germans expressed great interest in the political economies of both the Soviet Union and the United States. At that time, for many self-

proclaimed modernists, there existed a utopian and sometimes contradictory enthusiasm for elements of both capitalism and socialism, a desire to have the best of both worlds. This desire often played out in romantic images of technology and industry as societal curatives. Cutting across the Weimar political spectrum, this technological romanticism is central to Germany's political heritage, and the visual expression of these technological utopias has been a legacy for us in the United States as well, in terms of the way capitalism and corporations are represented and sold. We need only think of our most classic corporate identity programs, such as Paul Rand's original logo and graphics for IBM, to see how pervasive modernist utopian design has become. Here, I examine the utopian images and the politics of modernist advertising designers in the Weimar Republic, in particular, the practices of one leading trade group, the Circle of New Advertising Designers, as they called themselves—*NWG* or ring "*neue werbegestalter.*"[1]

Founded by Kurt Schwitters in 1928, the *neue werbegestalter* included artists who, like Schwitters, are known today through their fine arts: Willi Baumeister, Walter Dexel, the de Stijl painter Friedrich Vordemberge-Gildewart, the Dutch painter and photomontagist César Domela. All of these artists were deeply committed as well to commercial design work. Also in the group were artists who were well known as designers: Jan Tschichold, Max Burchartz, Georg Trump, Hans Leistikow, Robert Michel, and the leading Dutch modernists Piet Zwart and Paul Schuitema (fig. 3.1).

Schwitters energetically propagated advertising design in general and the works of neue werbegestalter members in particular. From 1928 to 1931, members of the ring seem to have been exhibiting constantly: they usually had two collections of works touring Germany and the Netherlands. For example, in 1928 one collection went from Köln to Wiesbaden to Barmen to Bochum to Hannover and another traveling exhibition went from Hamburg to Rotterdam to Halle.[2] In addition to requesting these core sets of graphics, Schwitters would write members to send additional and up-to-date works to various stops. Although Schwitters was the driving organizational force, all matters were scrupulously decided by group votes through the mail. Designers petitioning to join the *ring* would submit ten works that would circulate by post among the far-flung group. Then a vote would be taken. The group was generally inclusive, and although there was some wariness of being seen as an adjunct association of the Bauhaus, it often invited Bauhaus members to exhibit with them such as László Moholy-Nagy, Herbert Bayer, and Joost Schmidt (fig. 3.2). Other guests included John Heartfield from Berlin and Karl Tiege from Prague.[3]

Stylistically, the ring graphics are marked by a devotion to new typography and photomontage. Whereas in the early Weimar years photomontage was employed most often as a technique by the Berlin Dadaists (with a few toned-down examples in commercial advertising), by the late 1920s it was widely used in the mass media and had become a sign of the most modern style in graphics. By the late Weimar period,

Piet Zwart, *Voor biljde dagen geluktelegrammen*, graphics for PTT (The Dutch Telephone and Telegraph Company), photomontage, ca. 1929. Courtesy of Ex Libris Gallery, New York. **(3.1)**

Herbert Bayer, cover, *Bauhaus*, no. 1 (1928). Courtesy of the
Bauhaus Archiv, Berlin.
(**3.2**)

For Love, Modernism, or Money

the combination of modernist typography and photomontage in utilitarian design had several functions: an association with high art, an evocation of rationalization, and an alliance with internationalism. Photomontage in its various guises in high and mass culture was believed to represent a specifically modernist practice of seeing and experiencing.

With proselytizing zeal, ring members published in the modernist periodicals *Die Form* and *neue frankfurt*, where functionalist advertising design was promoted along with functionalist architecture. The ring "neue werbegestalter" was involved, too, in the formulation of the major 1931 international *Fotomontage* exhibition in Berlin, which included the former Berlin Dadaists John Heartfield, Hannah Höch, and Raoul Hausmann and key Soviet photomontagists. It was organized by ring member César Domela, who remarked about the opportunity the role provided him to invite the Soviets, Germans, and Dutch to exhibit together.[4] The NWG was also behind the publication of the 1930 book *Gefesselter Blick* (meaning literally "chained gaze" or, more metaphorically, "a fascinated and firmly focused gaze"). *Gefesselter Blick* was edited by the brothers Heinz and Bodo Rasch, and it can be seen as the most important survey of both advertising design and the accompanying manifestos of the period.[5]

Given the central, even pivotal, role of the ring in Weimar visual culture and its bridge position between high and low culture—avant-garde and mass culture—it is surprising how much the ring "neue werbegestalter" has been written out of art history. However, given traditional art history's function in the devaluing of mass culture and in the shoring up of an elite art market, and given leftist art history's tendency to look for "pure" and idealized heroes like John Heartfield, it is perhaps not so surprising. The ring makes an unlikely group of heroes or villains. The members' lives and production cannot be so reductively described. They were negotiating meaning and representation within several major arenas: capitalist advertising, mass communications, and, for some, leftist activism. This broad and sometimes contradictory range of activity is precisely why they are a significant object of study and questioning. The practices of different members varied. Some espoused Left radical politics, many admired and borrowed from Russian Constructivism—and at the same time served capitalist industry with great enthusiasm. Theirs were cultural practices within the nonrevolutionary societies of 1920s Holland and Germany. Their utopian visions, infused with a technological romanticism, espoused rationalized production and communication techniques. These visions dovetailed with a common desire among artists of the time to work hand in hand with an enlightened proletariat to build a greatly improved, more equitable society with a truly modern standard of living.

In fact, European culture in general in the 1920s demonstrated high expectations—across the political spectrum—for the societal effects of scientific management and technology. Postwar Europe embraced Taylorism, the time and labor efficiency tenets propagated by Friedrich W. Taylor in the United States before World War I. As historian Charles Maier explains, "By the 1920s, scientific management—which extended the original approaches of Taylorism into all areas of labor productivity, technological efficiency, and even corporate organization—evoked enthusiasm among European emulators as 'a characteristic feature of American civilization.'"[6] Scientific management promised the elimination of scarcity through surplus productivity, and this vision of plenty was quickly incorporated into both right-wing authoritarian models for government and socialist dreams for a classless society and individual welfare.[7] In the Soviet Union, Lenin early endorsed Taylorism, claiming rationalized labor was not exploitative if workers themselves profited.[8] In Germany, liberals such as Walter Rathenau and Georg Bernhard were interested in applying rationalization to government supervision of capitalist industry—efficiently yet autocratically setting prices, allocating raw material, and so on. Ultimately this type of rationalized practice found its way into the 1919 Weimar constitution in a compromised form as an advisory board, the Reichswirtschaftsrat (Reich Economic Council).[9] During the period of economic stabilization (1923–28), German industry became occupied with reorganizing the productive process through installing assembly lines and using advertising to aim at a mass consumer market.

With rationalization of production bearing the stamp of both U.S. and Soviet practice, the representation of rationalized technology in German culture often avoided any explicit political identification and,

Jan Tschichold, *Die Frau ohne Namen*
(The Woman without a Name), offset
lithograph poster, 1927. Collection of
Merrill C. Berman.
**(3.3)**

instead, focused on technical apparatus. In addition, divisions between
workers and management were elided by the mythic creation of the celebrated engineer, an amalgam of labor and management: creator, producer, thinker, doer—above all, efficient man.

Graphic designer and ring member Jan Tschichold introduces his influential 1928 book *Die Neue Typographie* by lauding the new man. He writes:

The works of today, untainted by the past, primary shapes which identify the
countenance of our time: Car Airplane Telephone Radio Neon New York!  These
objects have been created by a new kind of man: *the engineer!*

This engineer is the creator of our time. To characterize his works: economy, precision, composition from pure, constructive forms whose shape corresponds to function. Nothing is more characteristic of our time than these witnesses to the inventive genius of the engineer: Airport, Factory, Subway-car. These are standard forms: Typewriter, Lightbulb or Motorcycle.[10]

Tschichold, Weimar Germany's most well known promoter of New Typography, equates standardization and geometric form: "The constructive building of engineer-works and standard products led, of necessity, to the use of exact geometric forms. The final and most pure form of a necessary item is always constructed of geometric shapes."[11] Thus geometric form and grid composition in 1920s German graphics connoted such admiration of rationalization and technology, and a belief in the supreme importance of industry to society (a belief held by supporters of quite different governmental forms). The focus on form paralleled the fascination with means of production and both, it seems, worked together to block discussion among cultural modernists about industrial ownership, labor practices, and profits. This elision is particularly striking—and with hindsight, curious—among those who were actually producing advertisements for industry.

Jan Tschichold offers an interesting case of such omissions and contradictions (fig. 3.3). The designer, who admired the Soviet revolution to the point of signing his 1920s work Ivan (or Iwan) Tschichold, and who was influenced formally by Russian Constructivism, could enthuse about the engineer and standardization and could analyze the formal aspects of modern design and new typography without asking the attendant sociological questions about the function of his own corporate advertising within capitalism.[12] However, the focus on form during the 1920s was not about willful ignorance or disinterest in social issues, but rather part of inflated hopes for the ability of new technology (as it functioned in industry) and the new man (as personified by the engineer) to provide a new, more equitable society.

Maier asserts that the balloon of these dreams was punctured by the harsh conditions of the worldwide depression and that disillusionment

Paul Schuitema, *Workers' Demonstration*, vintage photograph, ca. 1932. Courtesy of Prof. Dr. Piet Zwart, Jr.
(**3.4a**)

Paul Schuitema, *Opfer vom polizeivorgehen gegen die protestkundgebung von arbeitsen in Rotterdam* (Victims of police brutality against the protests of the unemployed in Rotterdam), photograph, Dec. 22, 1932. Collection Prentenkabinet der Rijksuniveritat Leiden, Nederland.
(**3.4b**)

with rationalization followed, but this cannot be seen in German depression advertising. Quite the contrary—the claims became even more utopian, even grandiose, and the promotion of rationalization more strenuous.[13] And it is in this context that the popularity of the neue werbegestalter designers with their industrial clients (be they producers of steel, communications, stationery, or storage tanks) can be understood. The status of ring designers can be quickly conveyed by citing examples of high-visibility clients such as Kurt Schwitters's client, the city of Stuttgart; Max Burchartz's Bochumer Verein steel works; César Domela's the city of Hamburg; Willi Baumeister's the cultural magazine *Der Querschnitt*; and Piet Zwart's the Dutch postal service. In addition to industrial and government clients, ring designers were also frequently hired by museums, exhibition halls, and art book publishers. In neue werbegestalter graphics, the common style was to enclose photomontages within a constructivist grid, thus eliciting—yet firmly and "scientifically" containing—the speed and blur of an experience of modernity, the everyday assimilation of modern urban and technological imagery.

In the work of the Dutch designers Paul Schuitema and Piet Zwart, apparently conflicting political practices are reconciled through a utopian belief in rationalized technology. Schuitema and Zwart's activism in leftist politics has been well researched by the Dutch scholar Flip Bool.[14] The two photographer/designers, both based in Rotterdam, were members of the Union of Worker Photography. Both documented workers' demonstrations and clashes between workers and police (fig. 3.4a, b).[15] Schuitema designed new typography and photomontage covers for the periodicals *Links Richten* and *De Wapens Neder*, Zwart for leftist books such as *Wij Slaven von Suriname* by the revolutionary Anton de Kom (fig. 3.5). In addition, Schuitema wrote pseudonymously for *Links Richten*, most notably in his February 1933 article "Photography as a weapon in class war" (fig. 3.6).

Oddly, Schuitema uses the same language—that of rationalization—both to promote the training of worker-photographers and to extol advertising for capitalist industry. A reading of this language illustrates his elision of the contradictions of his two practices. On worker-photography, he writes: "No romanticism, no art, rather *sachlich*, glaringly suggestive propaganda: aligned tactically with the class war, technically with the trade."[17]  On advertising he writes in *Gefesselter Blick*: "Advertising should be: real, direct, *sachlich*, competitive, argumentative, active, contemporary, functional, practical, and technical—not art, but rather reality!" He continues in what seems to be an effort to unify different kinds of propaganda: "Advertising is neither art nor design. . . . It has no other purpose than to propagate man's material as well as spiritual production."[18]

Piet Zwart, *Umschlagentwurf für Anton de Kom,* Wij Slaven von Suriname, photocollage, 1934. Courtesy of the Haags Gemeentemuseum, Den Haag, The Netherlands.
**(3.5)**

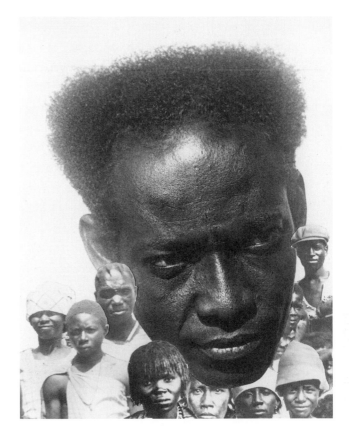

What Schuitema's attitudes toward the workers' movement and toward industrial advertising had in common was that he considered the rationalized means of production to be progressive and the communication process to be a natural extension of factory production. That the factories were owned by capitalists and that advertising contributed to their profits was completely left out of his and other ring designer's writings. The focus of the discourse was on the means of modern mass communi-

Paul Schuitema, cover, *Links Richten,* no. 1 (1932). Private collection.
(**3.6**)

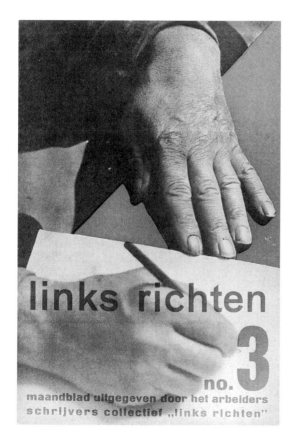

For Love, Modernism, or Money

cation, not on what was communicated. At the time, the only periodical in which these contradictions were pointed out was *Der Arbeiter-Fotograf* (The Worker-Photographer), in which the critic Alfred Kémeny protested the seemingly apolitical nature of advertising photomontages and labeled the images as "outright propaganda for the capitalist system."[19] Kémeny's article is one of a number in *Der Arbeiter-Fotograf* that sought to distinguish revolutionary photomontage, particularly John Heartfield's, from voguish photomontage in commercial advertising.

The close relationship Schuitema desired between his own designs and rationalized production can be illustrated by the artist's working method, which he attempted to make systematic, impersonal, and closely connected to mechanical production. In the Leiden University Print Cabinet, there are scrapbooks full of industrial photographs taken by Schuitema.[20] When he received an advertising commission from a company, for example the scale manufacturer Toledo-Berkel, he would docu-

Kurt Schwitters, cover, *Typoreklame, Merz* 11 (1924). Courtesy of Ex Libris Gallery, New York.
**(3.7)**

ment as thoroughly as possible all steps of production using unpopulated shots of machinery. He would then select from among these photographs the raw material for his advertising photomontages. These were not New Vision photographs but rather straight, midrange shots with a semblance of objectivity. The photomontages were to be a technical achievement, a modern filmic series of visual juxtapositions, not personal expression.

Talking of artists' intentions and discussing their formal products are, though, two separate and different kinds of analyses. Elsewhere I have written about the reified utopianism of Schwitters's designs with their adherence to the asymmetric block compositions of International Constructivism and the representation of the future as an antiseptic version of the present (fig. 3.7).[21] To analyze the questions of utopianism in conjunction with the ring's formal designs, I use Ernst Bloch's definition of utopianism as "anticipatory consciousness," or traces (*Spuren*) found in the present that inspire images of a desired future, a sort of epistemological montage. In Bloch's terms, then, visual montage is an appropriate vehicle for representing utopianism since its juxtaposition of fragments allows for a blossoming of allegory—providing multiple jumping-off points in the present from which to imagine a better future.[22] Nevertheless, it could be argued that many of the montages of the neue werbegestalter, however imaginative and technically proficient they may be, are limited in the types of allegories they allow to flower: these images prompt fables of zeppelins, bridges, linoleum rolls, and machine parts. The viewing subject extrapolated from the many viewpoints is merely a rationalized viewer of narrowly defined modern scenes and goods.

At this point one might ask cynically if all the exhibiting, promoting, and fervent talk about the blessings of advertising on the part of the ring artists was not simply a desperate attempt to earn a living at commercial graphics during the worldwide depression. This, after all, is how traditional art histories have described the involvement of a fine artist like Schwitters in commercial advertising. However, one has only to read the ring members' published statements and their letters to one another to realize how much more than money was at stake: these documents are evidence of a serious desire to contribute to mass culture, to sway it

For Love, Modernism, or Money

toward functionalism, rationality, and a glorifying of production. Within this chapter, I want to develop a history of the ring and its colleagues that concentrates on these issues of intentionality, to help define the neue werbegestalter and to make sense of the group's undocumented primary sources. Most important, a greater insight into their self-definitions will bring us to a revised understanding of the term "historical avant-garde."

The belief system of the group as a whole can be quickly surveyed by analyzing their manifesto-like statements in the book *Gefesselter Blick* (fig. 3.8a,b,c). There, the ideal of rationalized production is applied to modern seeing; thus, the creation and viewing of photomontages is described as an intelligent assembling of parts to allow for a rational, efficient consumption. Walter Dexel writes that modern man has the right to expect communications in the shortest possible time. Willi

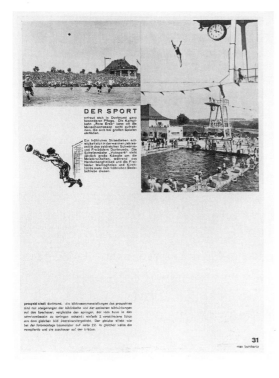

Willi Baumeister, cover, *Gefesselter Blick,* ed. Heinz and Bodo Rasch (Stuttgart: Verlag Dr. Zaugg and Co., 1930). Courtesy of Kunstbibliothek, Staatliche Museen, Preussischer Kulturbesitz, Berlin. (**3.8a**)

Max Burchartz, *6 Millionen Fahrkarten— Prospekt für die Stadt Dortmund* (6 Million Tickets—Brochure for the city of Dortmund) in *Gefesselter Blick,* ed. Heinz and Bodo Rasch (Stuttgart: Verlag Dr. Zaugg and Co., 1930), 29. Courtesy of Kunstbibliothek, Staatliche Museen, Preussischer Kulturbesitz, Berlin. (**3.8b**)

Max Burchartz, *Der Sport—Prospekt für die Stadt Dortmund* (Sport—Brochure for the city of Dortmund) in *Gefesselter Blick,* ed. Heinz and Bodo Rasch (Stuttgart: Verlag Dr. Zaugg and Co., 1930), 31. Courtesy of Kunstbibliothek, Staatliche Museen, Preussischer Kulturbesitz, Berlin. (**3.8c**)

Baumeister points out that photomontage is efficient, allowing for the quick grasp of several images at once. The Rasch brothers in their introduction cite rationalization as the paradigm for advertising. Dexel insists on creating clarity, not beauty. It seems ironic that in a search for rationality and clarity these designers should end up with photomontage and its kaleidoscopic imagery. Domela uses a travel analogy as well as a filmic one to describe his photomontages. Similarities between photomontage and film are often emphasized, with photomontage being considered a quicker, more efficient medium. Finally, the overriding message of the manifestos in *Gefesselter Blick* is an enthusiasm for advertising, new technology, and mass communication.

To consider the specific utopianism of the neue werbegestalter is to analyze a set of images that represent certain processes of modernization

For Love, Modernism, or Money

during the Weimar period. These are utopian representations of rationalization and its effects. Images closely tied to the factory (images of mass production, advanced technology, new possibilities of scale) are combined with other images meant to suggest the interiorization of rationalization in the viewer, or, simply put, man as machine. This, in turn, leads to new possibilities for perception. Yet, certain images common to Weimar consumer culture, those associated with women, are few in ring images.

In the 1920s, mass culture, particularly film and advertising, was considered the province of women. In Germany, as in the United States, most advertising was aimed at women who, it was widely acknowledged, did most of the purchasing of goods. Mass cultural products such as the illustrated newspapers that depended on consumer advertising were full of images of Weimar's New Woman, multifaceted symbol of modernity. In general, much mass-cultural imagery represented and/or was aimed at women. New Woman images often connoted gender ambiguity and the possibility of change in traditional gender roles. (In fact, the term "New Woman" was not just a symbolic one. The Weimar woman differed from her pre–World War I counterpart in that she now held the vote and probably had fewer children; in addition, she was more likely to be working for a wage, to have had an illegal abortion, to be married, to work in a pink-collar position or in a newly rationalized industry, and to live in a city.)

But the New Woman is scarcely evident in the advertising of the neue werbegestalter, which tends to focus on production and modes of perception rather than on consumption. The neue werbegestalter graphics generally offer many of the familiar signs of modernity—the grid; photomontage; new typography; images of up-to-date, mass-produced objects—but usually omit the ubiquitous image of the New Woman. The designers' intention—one paralleled by their clients' interest—was to promote technology and a rationalized modernity.[23] Their clients were primarily heavy industry like steel, or communications systems like the post office, and were not likely to include producers of clothes, food, personal hygiene items, or domestic goods.

The ring's approach is a particularly masculinist approach to photomontage and mass culture, deemphasizing ambiguity, identifying heavily with mechanical production, ignoring almost completely the feminine-gendered world of consumerism, and, not incidentally, including no women as members of the ring, not even Grete Leistikow who often worked collaboratively with her brother Hans, a member. While contemporaneous artists such as Hannah Höch used ambiguity in their photomontages to construct allegories and confound fixed notions of gender, and theorists such as Ernst Bloch stressed connections between montage, allegory, and ambiguity, the neue werbegestalter in their writings emphasized their desire for just the opposite characteristic in their montages: clarity.

Within this masculinist frame of reference, how is clarity attributed to photomontage? Above all, this connection is established through analogies to science and technology. (Although some Weimar cultural representations like the film *Metropolis* show technology as *embodied* by woman, most often the *employment* of technology is gendered as masculine.) Clarity, for the ring, is not reduction, but instead high-quality production. It is offering a smorgasbord of modern imagery so that the viewer can assimilate it with sophisticated speed. Perhaps there is an unspoken desire for ambiguity as well; both Burchartz and Domela value the opportunity to provide multiple viewpoints that photomontage offers (fig. 3.9). Burchartz asserts that his works do not provide a controlled perspective but instead survey a rapid journey of urban impressions. However, these multiple viewpoints are contained and controlled by the compositional grid inspired by constructivism and the stark legibility demanded by advertising, so the modernism of the neue werbegestalter did not so much suggest change and flexibility as it did a rigid and anesthetized version of the future, offering through advertising and mass communications a masculinist avant-garde utopia for the masses.

In conclusion, I want to use this understanding of the ring to consider and revise a current definition of the historical avant-garde. Peter Bürger, in his *Theory of the Avant-Garde*, defines the 1920s European avant-garde by contrasting it with a previous tradition of aestheticism.[24] He calls the art-for-art's-sake practices "modernism." However, by the 1920s, the term "modernism" was no longer restricted to meaning a hermetic aestheticism. Culturally, "modernism" could refer to earlier art-for-art's-

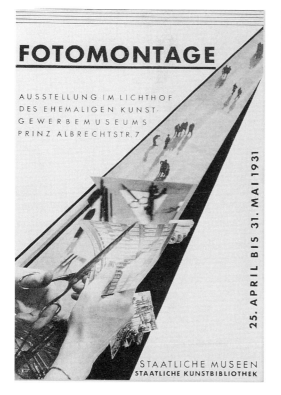

César Domela, cover, *Fotomontage* (Apr. 25–May 31, 1931), Berlin, 1931. Exhibition catalog. © 2000 Artists Rights Society (ARS), New York/ADAGP, Paris.
**(3.9)**

sake movements; but also, in Weimar Germany the term *Modernismus* had more powerful connotations due to its associations with the words *moderne* (modern, contemporary, fashionable) and *Modernität* (modernity, the experience of modernization). Although *Modernismus* could refer to an art movement such as Expressionism, it had a double use; it could also mean the culture of contemporary life and the experience of technology, electricity, urbanism, speed, mass media, and consumerism. For my purposes in considering the relationship between artists and mass culture, the multiple use of the term is significant.

As literary critics Andreas Huyssen and David Bathrick have argued, Bürger's theory "represses the largest truth about modernism itself— namely . . . the heterogeneity of its response to the maelstrom of modernization."[25] Still, Bürger is correct when he contrasts an avant-garde

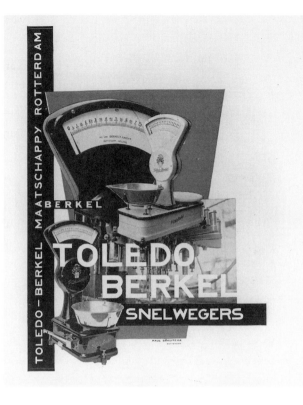

Paul Schuitema, *Proefdruk adresboek, Toledo-Berkel Mij*, in series of advertisements for Berkel, bookprint, undated. Courtesy of Haags Gemeentemuseum, Den Haag, The Netherlands.
**(3.10)**

group like Berlin Dada with earlier aesthetic movements; or to be more precise, Bürger's definition echoes their intentions. The avant-garde's goal, Bürger claims, was to rebel against the institutionalization of art in order to reengage art with life. Applying his definition to German culture, one finds that it functions as an apt, if incomplete, description of Berlin Dada with the latter's emphasis on provocative photomontage, anarchic performance, inclusive exhibitions, and political publications. However, Berlin Dada was a short-lived moment in the formation of the German avant-garde. The movement was completely over by 1922, and the burning issue for the German avant-garde from 1922 until Hitler's seizure of power in 1933 was not at all a rebellion against art institutions, but rather a serious and prolonged engagement with mass culture. This engagement was inspired in part by the practices of the much-admired

**For Love, Modernism, or Money**

Russian Constructivists. Photobooks, photographs for illustrated newspapers, trade-fair-like exhibitions, commercial design, book design, film—all these were not sidelines for the avant-garde but primary objects of production (fig. 3.10). And in this the artists of the ring "neue werbegestalter" are emblematic.

To exclude this involvement with mass communications from art history, as has been common practice, is to create a history in which artists and intellectuals are sequestered from the majority of society—from societal evolution, discourse, and change. It is, as in Kurt Schwitters's case, to mask an elaborate engagement with mass culture as merely a function of personal finances. To write such a repressed history is to suggest that artists have been and should be restricted to producing only for one another and in reaction to one another. Such isolation was not the condition of a 1920s avant-garde deeply occupied with mass-cultural production. Nor need isolation from mass culture and its societal issues be a scholarly or artistic condition today. Connotatively, ring "neue werbegestalter" images evoke a political admixture of capitalism and socialism, promote a technological romanticism, often convey a corporate identity, and imply a masculine experience. The historical avant-garde of which they were a part, then, should be understood not solely in terms of politically heroic figures such as John Heartfield. Instead, a more nuanced cultural history is called for, one that recognizes that these and other 1920s artists endeavored for ideological and financial reasons to reach a mass audience and to participate fully in modern means of communication. To focus as a cultural historian on the political and formal ambiguities of their project is to open the door to a fuller understanding of the historical avant-garde's contemporary legacy, encompassing as it does extremely diverse utopias and images. Contemporary involvements of artists with design projects can be analyzed not reductively in terms of adding to the canon of artistic heroes, but more broadly in terms of cultural and sociological issues—the functions and efficacy of the graphics. Consider the different audiences and different means of presentation of feminist artists such as Jenny Holzer, who have employed mass-media images to explore issues of identity and address; of mediawise activist graphics such as the AIDS images of Gran Fury, which are so effective at reaching a mass audience; and of the rationalized corporate identity programs that flood our culture, such as Chermayeff/Geismar's anesthetized graphics for Mobil corporation. Unlike elitist art histories that, when they address mass culture at all, focus narrowly on fine artists who take their "inspiration" from mass culture, I would like to direct cultural criticism to these areas where the intersection of art and mass culture carries with it issues of societal urgency and engagement.

**Notes**

1. ring *"neue werbegestalter"* is the spelling and capitalization used by the group, as evidenced by their letterhead, designed by Kurt Schwitters.

2. A complete list of the exhibitions of the ring "neue werbegestalter" was compiled in the exhibition catalog "Typografie kann unter Umständen Kunst sein": Ring 'neue werbegestalter' Die Amsterdamer Ausstellung 1931 (Wiesbaden: Landesmuseum Wiesbaden, 1990), 141: 25.3–22.4.1028 Kunstgewerbemuseum Köln; Juni 1928 Museum Wiesbaden; Sept./Okt. 1928 Kunstverein Barmen; Okt. 1928 Museum für Kunst und Gewerbe, Hamburg; Dez. 1928 Bochum; Dez. 1928 Academie von Beeldende Kunsten, Rotterdam Anfang 1929 Halle; Jan. 1929 Provinzialmuseum Hannover; 10.3–23.3.1929 Haghaus, Bremen; 20.4–20.5.1929 Staatliche Bibliothek, Berlin; 21.4–29.4.1929 Neue Kunst Fides, Dresden; Mai 1929 Kunstverein Heilbronn; 18.5–7.7.1929 Stuttgart; 3.8–19.8.1929 Ausstellungshalen am Adolf-Mittag-See, Magdeburg; 22.9–[unknown] 1929 Museum Folkwang, Essen 8.–11.2.1930 Stuttgart; 30.3–27.4.1930 Gewerbemuseum Basel; 3.4–6.4.1930 Graphische Gesellschaft, München; o. D. 1930 Kopenhagen; o. D. 1930 Aarau 3.–6.4.1931 Stockholm; 30.5–5.6.1931 Ausstellungshallen, Essen; 20.6–12.7.1931 Stedelijk Museum, Amsterdam.

3. See circular and personal letters from Kurt Schwitters to Piet Zwart, archive number 850831, Archives of the History of Art, The Getty Center for the History of Art and the Humanities, Los Angeles. I would like to thank Pamela Johnston of the Archives for making these accessible to me. The letters are published in part in the Wiesbaden neue werbegestalter catalog.

4. César Domela letter to the author, Paris, Dec. 12, 1989.

5. *Gefesselter Blick: 25 Kurze Monografien und Beiträge über neue Werbegestaltung*, ed. Heinz und Bodo Rasch (Stuttgart: Verlag Dr. Zaugg and Co., 1930).

6. Charles S. Maier, "Between Taylorism and Technocracy: European Ideologies and the Vision of Industrial Productivity in the 1920s," *The Journal of Contemporary History* 5, no. 2 (1970): 27.

7. For an examination of technological romanticism on the right, see Jeffrey Herf, *Reactionary Modernism: Technology, Culture, and Politics in Weimar and the Third Reich* (Cambridge: Cambridge University Press, 1982).

8. Scientific management was an idea that took deep root in the Soviet Union and was abused in the first Five Year Plan, implemented in 1928, with its excessive production quotas. Judith A. Merkle, *Management and Ideology: The Legacy of the International Scientific Management Movement* (Berkeley: University of California Press, 1980), 121–124.

9. Charles S. Maier, "Between Taylorism and Technocracy: European ideologies and the vision of industrial productivity in the 1920s," *The Journal of Contemporary History* 5, no. 2 (1970): 51.

10. "Ihr stehen heute jene Werke gegenüber, die, unbelastet durch Vergangenheit, primäre Erscheinungen, das Antlitz unserer Zeit bestimmt haben: Auto Flugzeug Telephon Radio Warenhaus Lichtreklame New York! Diese neuen Menschentyp geschaffen worden: *Dem Ingenieur!*

Dieser Ingenieur ist der Gestalter unseres Zeitalters. Kennzeichnen seiner Werke: Ökonomie, Präzision, Bildung aus reinen, konstruktiven Formen, die der funktion des Gegenstands entsprechen. Nichts, das bezeichnender für unsere Zeit wäre, als diese Zeugen des Erfindergeistes der Ingenieure, seien es Einzelleistungen: Flugplatz, Fabrikhalle, Triebwagen der Untergrund; seien es Standardformen: Schreibmaschine, Glühbirne oder Motorrad" (Jan Tschichold, *Die Neue Typografie* (Berlin: Brinkmann & Bose, 1987 [1928], 11)

11. "Der konstruktive Aufbau des Ingenieurwerke und Standardprodukte hat mit Notwendigkeit zum Gebrauch der exakten geometrischen Formen geführt. Die letzte und reinste Form eines Gebrauchsgegendstandes baut sich immer aus geometrischen Gebilden auf" (Jan Tschichold, *Die Neue Typografie* (Berlin: Brinkmann & Bose, 1987 [1928]), 12).

12. For biographical details, see Ruari McLean, *Jan Tschichold: Typographer* (Boston: David Godine, 1975), 35–37.

13. See chapter 4, this volume.

14. Flip Bool, "Paul Schuitema und Piet Zwart: Die Neue Typografie und Die Neue Fotografie im Dienst der Industrie und des politischen Kampfes," in *Avant Garde und Industrie*, ed. Stanislaus von Moos and Chris Smeenk (Delft: Delft University Press, 1983), 121–133.

15. A contextual note about Dutch economics and politics in the 1920s: At this time, the Netherlands was a parliamentary democracy with a constitutional monarchy (as it still is today). Like Germany, it was undergoing modernization, but at a slower pace. Although in 1917 some labor reforms had been enacted such as the eight-hour work-day, the fluctuating economy during the 1920s required continued labor vigilance and activism. The Netherlands was hard hit by the depression.

16. S. Palsma, "Foto also wapen in de klassestrijk," *Links Richten* (Feb. 1933).

17. As quoted and translated by Flip Bool in "Paul Schuitema und Piet Zwart: Die Neue Typografie und die Neue Fotografie im Dienste der Industrie und des politischen

Kampfes" in *Avant Garde und Industrie,* ed. Stanislaus von Moos and Chris Smeenk (Delft: Delft University Press, 1983), 122: "Keine Romantik, keine Kunst, sondern sachliche, grell suggestive Propaganda: Taktisch auf den Klassenkampf, technisch auf das Fach ausgerichtet."

18. As quoted in *Gefesselter Blick,* ed. Heinz and Bodo Rasch (Stuttgart: Verlag Dr. Zaugg and Co., 1930): ". . . reklame [sic] soll sein: reell, direkt, sachlich, konkurrenzfähig, argumentierend, aktiv, aktuell, funktionell, praktisch und technisch, keine Kunst, sondern Wirklichkeit! . . . Reklame ist weder Kunst noch Gestaltung. . . . sie hat kein andern Zweck als materielle sowie geistige Produktion des Menschen zu propagieren."

19. Kémeny applies this criticism to a photomontage captioned "Hamburg, Germany's gate to the world." He does not name the artist who created the photomontage, but it was probably done by Domela who produced advertising for the city of Hamburg. Alfred Kémeny wrote pseudonymously as Durus. Durus, "Fotomontage, Fotogramm," *Der Arbeiter-Fotograf* 5, no. 7 (1931): 166–168, in *Photography in the Modern Era,* ed. Christopher Phillips (New York: The Metropolitan Museum of Art/Aperture, 1989), 183.

20. Leiden University Print Cabinet, Paul Schuitema Book 1: PS1–178.

21. Maud Lavin, "Advertising Utopia: Schwitters as Commercial Designer," *Art in America* 73, no. 10 (Oct. 1985): 134–139, 169.

22. Ernst Bloch, *The Utopian Function of Art and Literature,* trans. Jack Zipes and Frank Mecklenburg (Cambridge, Mass.: MIT Press, 1988).

23. Today, corporate designers have much less to say about the content of advertising than apparently did the ring "neue werbegestalter" designers. It would be inappropriate, therefore, in any discussion of contemporary advertising to focus so exclusively on the designers' intentions as I do in this essay; a cultural history project would be better informed by examining the intersection of the designers' intentions with the corporate clients' goals. However, the neue werbegestalter were considered advertising artists. Their work was exhibited in museums. They seem to have had a great deal of say about the look and content of their commercial work, as evidenced in part by quite similar images produced for different clients.

24. Peter Bürger, *Theory of the Avant-Garde,* trans. Michael Shaw (Minneapolis.: University of Minnesota Press, 1984).

25. Andreas Huyssen and David Bathrick, "Modernism and the Experience of Modernity," in *Modernity and the Text: Revisions of German Modernism,* ed. Andreas Huyssen and David Bathrick (New York: Columbia University Press, 1989), 8.

# ringl + pit:

## The Representation of Women
## in German Advertising, 1929–33

During the depression, German advertising promoted a vision of a technological utopia and promised an improved lifestyle based on consuming
mass-produced commodities. It represented the machine and its products
as reassuring instruments of security and control. Photography played a
complex role in constructing this vision, a vision so idealized that an advertising page would rarely include a photograph unless it were heavily
retouched.

Within this framework, advertising's representation of women was
problematic. Women were advertising's primary market; in 1932 the
German advertising trade journal *Gebrauchsgraphik* estimated that 85 percent of
all commodities were bought by women.[1] Statistics were similar in the
United States, and historians of early American advertising have analyzed its
pressures on women to consider themselves foremost as rational consumers.[2] In German advertisements during this period of economic crisis, however, women appeared not only as consumers
but also, less predictably, as idealized, machine-made commodities, at times portrayed literally as manikins. These
observations raise large questions about advertising's representation of women, how it both promulgated and restricted myths about Weimar Germany's New Woman, and what
this might have meant for female viewers.

Particularly relevant to these issues is the collaborative work of two female photographers, Ellen Auerbach and Grete Stern, and their commercial studio, Foto ringl + pit. For although the two usually worked within the advertising system and enjoyed a marginal commercial success, they deviated significantly from the accepted conventions of representing women. Not only did they refrain from equating women with commodities, but through creating humorous and nostalgic masquerades they also developed alternative images of femininity.

If ringl + pit's work can be considered different, what then were German advertising's standard images of women and common photographic styles? During the twenties, in both the United States and Europe, advertising achieved a large distribution in conjunction with the growth of mass-media periodicals. Simultaneous with this proliferation in Germany, advertising's bid for the female consumer was informed by major changes in women's social status, shifts that earned the Weimar generation the title of New Women. Women had just gained the right to vote in late 1918, the birth rate was declining gradually, and the number of women working was slowly rising. During the depression, a conservative reaction feared women active outside the home, particularly in the workplace.[3] Although advertising sought to attract female viewers, it did not simply generate positive images of women. Rather, advertising images were complex representations of the anxieties and desires concerning new identities for women in Weimar Germany. In these ads, women were addressed as "empowered" buyers, but often only insofar as their power was limited to purchasing products that would enable them to construct themselves—through make-up, shampoo, powder—as exchangeable objects, commodities. Women in so many of these images look perfect, machine-made.

Photography participated in advertising's representation of woman as commodity by providing several options for idealization and fetishization.[4] The most acceptable style for advertising photography was a heavily retouched one that connoted both art (in its similarity to advertising graphics) and document (in its resemblance to photojournalism, supposedly in a machine-made record). This ambiguity is emphasized in advertising page layouts where the photograph is often used to bridge a graphic

ringl + pit

scene of a utopian lifestyle and a separate image of a machine-made product, as can be seen in two examples.

In a 1930 *Die Dame* Agfa camera ad, the composite image shows a woman on a sailboat photographing a regatta further out on the water.[5] The woman photographing is drawn, not photographed. She is secure and flawless; she is fashionably dressed; her dog sits comfortably next to her. Above her, but in her line of sight, is the view she is seeing/has photographed: the scene is light, airy, and unruffled, and the retouching emphasizes the play of light on the water. The photograph's composition and its placement on the page (upper right) signify control and balance. It is ostensibly her photograph, her production, but it looms over and behind her like a movie screen. Her back is to us; she is more spectator than producer. The image suggests pleasure, vacation, the exotic, wealth, the movies. The only area of the page, besides text, that is not "drawn" (either a sketch or a retouched photograph) is the cut-out image of the camera in the lower right corner. If the other images with their handcrafted elements signify art, then the crispness of this image identifies the camera as a machine. The photographic image of the Agfa camera, the product, is seemingly not retouched; it functions as a signature, author of both the sailing image and the pleasurable, controlled lifestyle. A 1929 *Berliner Illustrirte* [sic] *Zeitung* ad for Pixavon shampoo (fig. 4.1) also situates the photograph (soft focus, retouched, signed) between the idealized art image (a drawing of a mother and child) and the modern product (the shampoo), and again the product is the author of the woman's accession to an ideal.[6]

A less common photographic style in advertising was a modernist one that pictured stark, monumentalized commodities, one that illustrated a reverence for the formal beauty of machine-made objects and for photography as mechanical reproduction. In this category are Hans Finsler's repeated rows of gleaming porcelain cups and Walter Peterhans's advertising photography. Bauhaus-trained artists often worked within this style, and Auerbach and Stern complied with what were essentially modernist standards. Both had studied with the Bauhaus photography professor Walter Peterhans (Stern from 1927 to 1930, Auerbach from 1928 to

*A New Profession: The Sound Controller*, cover, *Berliner
Illustrirte Zeitung* (Aug. 11, 1929). Courtesy of the General
Research Division, The New York Public Library, Astor, Lenox
and Tilden Foundations.

**(4.2)**

1930). Although this style would seem to oppose the common use of heavily retouched photography, both can be read as idealized, with the most significant difference between the two styles being the ways in which, in the modernist photographs, this idealization is aligned more directly with the machine and industry.

Although this formal style is now generally associated with art photography and the Bauhaus, at the time it also appealed to advertising's need—urgent during the depression—to monumentalize and revere industrial objects, for corporations to represent industry as a way to an improved life. (Despite some socialist intentions with which the Weimar Republic had been born in 1918, the Weimar era economic system was capitalist.) The function of straight, formalist photography for advertising was to provide reassurance. This was emphasized repeatedly in contemporary advertising trade journals. For instance, in 1931, *Gebrauchsgraphik* praised Hans Finsler's corporate advertising photography for the confidence and joy it communicated:

Consider the pictures for the North German Lloyd [steamer]. The monumental exaggeration of the gigantic ship's hull attracts us magnetically, forcefully towards it. The rounded, comfortable bows of the projecting lifeboat with its dark coat of iron plates inform us with a sense of trust and confidence, the noble curve of the white decks or the mysterious charm of a cloud looming up in the distance lure us to far foreign journeys. These pictures have an indefinable atmosphere. A strong and vital feeling of joy in life streams from them and imparts itself to the beholder. That is why they are so convincing, and at the same time such remarkably good advertising.[7]

This attitude was evident in photojournalism as well. The August 11, 1929, *Berliner Illustrirte Zeitung* cover (fig. 4.2) also uses photography to represent technology, control, and monumentality, and these in turn are aligned, as the caption announces, with hope for new employment: "A new profession: the sound controller"—all of which speaks to Germany's spiraling unemployment at the time.

In this context of advertising ideology, deviations by Auerbach and Stern from commercial photography standards—which seem minor when viewed only in stylistic terms—have a much greater significance. Although the ringl + pit work can be categorized roughly as Bauhaus photography, with its fascination with form and texture and its stylistic leanings toward either straight photography or montage, Auerbach and Stern did not engage in monumentalizing commodities to the same degree as Peterhans. They rarely used melodramatic lighting, and they avoided repetition, which is so embedded in photography's fetishizing function. To examine ringl + pit's photography is to question it as intervention from within prevailing commercial and modernist systems. Their work was published as advertising and praised as art. However, within these systems, Auerbach and Stern refused certain standards and created new devices. Specifically, their ironic criticism emerged in their representations of women. These responses were to a large extent predicated on their own experiences as New Women within Berlin upper-middle-class artistic/intellectual circles. In turn, their individual biographies are emblematic of widespread social changes for a whole generation of Weimar women.

Their backgrounds were similar: both Auerbach and Stern came from small-town, conventional, bourgeois Jewish families. And the degree of independence Auerbach and Stern established was tremendous in comparison to the standards with which they had been raised. Grete Stern was born in 1904 and grew up in Wuppertal-Elberfeld; Ellen Auerbach, born in 1906, was raised in Karlsruhe. Both trained in art schools, with Stern studying graphics at Kunstgewerbeschule Stuttgart from 1925 to 1927 and Auerbach sculpture at Karlsruher Kunstakademie (1924–27) and Kunstschule Stuttgart (1928). In 1927 Stern moved to Berlin to study with Walter Peterhans in an apprentice situation. Auerbach came to Berlin in 1928 to study photography with Peterhans, a decision due in part to the necessity of earning a living. In the late twenties Peterhans was commuting between Berlin and the Dessau Bauhaus, but by 1930 he decided to sell his Berlin studio and equipment to Stern, who had received a small inheritance. This was the point at which Stern and Auerbach officially opened their business, ringl + pit, named after their childhood nicknames (Stern—ringl, Auerbach—pit). In fact, they had been collaborating since 1928, together evolving their technical skills and producing still lifes and portraits. This mutual support extended beyond their professional lives; in 1930, when Auerbach's parents stopped sending her money, both she and the studio moved into Stern's apartment. There they formed a circle of friends, which included their future husbands Walter Auerbach and Horacio Coppola. Their relationships with friends and lovers, although conventional by today's standards, comprised a sharp break with the codes of conduct with which they had been raised.[8]

The new possibilities for women in Weimar affected the professional, political, social, and sexual lives of Auerbach and Stern—and influenced the production of their studio. This is not to suggest that their photography be considered simplistically as reflections or records of cultural changes, but rather that it be investigated in the context of its times for problems and issues raised for individual women as spectators and for Auerbach and Stern as artists.

With their images of women, Auerbach and Stern developed alternative representations within the advertising system, as evidenced by comparing the 1931 ringl + pit *Petrole Hahn* ad (fig. 4.3) with a Berlin Elizabeth Arden advertisement of the same year (fig. 4.4). In accordance with advertising's aims of empowering yet limiting the female buyer and picturing a technical, utopian world, women were aligned or equated with commodities. The Berlin Elizabeth Arden advertisement, for example, from a June 1931 *Die Dame* presents an image impossible to identify as either a person or a manikin.[9] There is no distance between the woman and the masquerade. In *Petrole Hahn* (1931), Auerbach and Stern both spoof and challenge this conflation of woman and manikin (or woman and commodity). Through humor and nostalgia, Auerbach and Stern distance the female masquerade from the female subject. The ringl + pit advertisement for Petrole Hahn hair shampoo portrays a smiling, wigged manikin wearing Auerbach's mother's nightgown, but the hand holding the bottle is a real human hand. It is a humor that reveals Auerbach's and Stern's discomfort with the manikin = woman equation, and a humor that disrupts that association for the viewer. Through humor, and with some confusion, the reader realizes which fragment is man-made and which is flesh,

**ringl + pit**

ringl + pit, *Petrole Hahn,* photograph, 1931. © ringl
+ pit. Courtesy of the Robert Miller Gallery, New
York.
**(4.3)**

*Predilection for White—and Which Make-Up?,*
advertisement for Elizabeth Arden, *Die Dame* (June
1931). Courtesy of the General Research Division,
The New York Public Library, Astor, Lenox and Tilden
Foundations.
**(4.4)**

Vorliebe für WEISS —
und welches Make-up?

ELIZABETH ARDEN
BERLIN W. LENNÉSTRASSE 5

NEW YORK      LONDON      PARIS      ROM

and a perfect melding of the two is disallowed. (Actually to use humor at all in German advertising at the time was transgressive; early German advertisements comprise a persistently serious body of images.) Further, the ringl + pit manikin is not a high-fashion type. On the pages of *Die Dame*, the manikins displaying fashion items are abstracted, sleek, with Art Nouveau-derived heads. They are ultramodern. In contrast, ringl + pit's manikin wears a nightgown from a previous generation, a nostalgia particularly out of place in advertising, with its promotion of the new and accordingly its use of photography to connote the new and technological.

Auerbach and Stern were female producers of photographs and also female consumers of mass-media images. In their work, we can see a focus on various types of feminine masquerade, a frequent theme in the media (think of the flagrantly androgynous film costumes of Marlene Dietrich and Asta Nielsen). Film theorist Mary Ann Doane has written about an exploration of the masquerade as a kind of antidote to the problems for women in identifying with an idealized female star who appears in movies as a fetish object. Doane outlines the equally negative choice for female viewers of either identifying narcissistically with an object of desire (becoming one's own object of desire) or overly identifying with an idealized and impossible female image as a destructively masochistic operation on one's identity. A way to avoid these negative options, Doane suggests, is to manipulate femininity (the cultural construct of the feminine) as a masquerade, therefore gaining control of and distance from the mask(s) of femininity.[10] Ringl + pit's refusal to depict women as commodities/manikins and their alternative emphasis on the artifice of this masquerade, then, can be read as exercising such control.

In addition to humor, Auerbach and Stern used other devices to exaggerate the masquerade. Their well-known *Komol* hair-dye ad (fig. 4.5) is a montage, literally a representational screen on and behind which a selection of dyed hair and the lines of a woman's face compose an image of stylish femininity. The use of montage prevents the reading of the woman's face as a seamless, natural image. It is self-consciously and humorously artificial. In other works, the masquerade is highlighted simply by focusing on its composition; two (noncommercial) versions of *Dancer Eckstein* (1930) show her applying lipstick and looking at her reflection in the mirror.

ringl + pit

ringl + pit, *Komol*, photograph, 1931. © ringl + pit. Courtesy of the
Robert Mann Gallery, New York.
(4.5)

Perhaps ringl + pit's most critical strategy, in addition to humor, is the invoking of nostalgia. At its sharpest, their nostalgia contributed to negative critiques of traditional women's roles such as the bride and the mother. *Fragment of a Bride* (1930) depicts a delicately lit, black-grounded piece of white tulle. An ironic comment, the photograph evidences the same fascination with form and texture as ringl + pit's still lifes, but the material is coarse—thus eliminating connotations of wealth—and frayed, cut, and fragmented—thus negating its ceremonial value. At other times, Auerbach and Stern create pleasurable masquerades using Auerbach's mother's clothes—photographs (both commercial and noncommercial) that hinge on complex attitudes toward generational differences and femininity. Auerbach remembers the pleasure she and Stern took in posing a friend for *Mother's Corset* (1929), a torso shot of a back dressed only in a corset:

It was my mother's corset. I took everything I liked that she had kept. The dress I wear in *Pit with Veil* is my mother's engagement dress. And in the *Petrole Hahn* and in the *Sleeping Girl*, the nightgown was a nightgown of my mother's. All this stuff that was made so carefully and so elaborately.[11]

*Mother's Corset* is in sharp focus, but it is lit for sensual, soft gray tones. Their friend's buttocks are visible beneath the corset, creating an erotic and—considering the generational differences on sexuality—rebellious image.

What does it mean that, in *Petrole Hahn* and *Mother's Corset*, femininity is portrayed nostalgically with the clothes of an earlier generation? Joan Riviere, writing in 1929, viewed the female masquerade as protective covering for those assuming "masculine" roles and actions, a reaction to so-called improper female behavior, hiding behind a mask of ultra-femininity:

women who wish for masculinity (or the "masculine" societal role of producer) may put on a mask of womanliness to avert anxiety and the retribution feared from men. . . . Womanliness therefore could be assumed and worn as a mask, both to hide the possession of masculinity and to avert the reprisals expected if she was found to possess it.[12]

**ringl + pit**

In the 1920s in Germany, to enter the workplace, to refuse or post-pone marriage, to not be mothers, all these behaviors (which describe Auerbach and Stern) could be considered masculine. It is no exaggeration to say that given the generational differences of the Weimar era, to a conventional woman of Auerbach's mother's generation, almost every element of Auerbach's and Stern's lives could appear deviant. When ringl + pit construct female masquerades to cover or deny elements of "masculinity" by using a mother's clothes, they create a camouflage that, although attractive, is clearly out-of-date. They use the mixed emotions of nostalgia to separate a traditional masquerade of femininity from other more alternative fantasies of identity.

Ringl + pit's work can be lauded for the powerful alternatives it presents for the representation of women, through humor, nostalgia, and masquerade. However, such images offer the possibility of particular interventions rather than an actual transformation of the advertising system. Certain images such as *Mother's Corset* were not made for sale. Others such as *Petrole Hahn* and *Komol* were sold to clients and published as advertisements. Although these are critical, many ringl + pit images merely evidence a partial refusal or balking at certain prevalent attitudes. For example, a jewelry dealer commissioned the studio, through their agent, to produce a photograph for a Mother's Day brochure.[13] The result was an uninspired photograph of their landlady, with her hair powdered white, receiving jewelry. The setup appears deliberately artificial and noncelebratory. In fact, Auerbach and Stern were unsympathetic to the institution of Mother's Day, which they viewed as a conservative holiday. Mother's Day, which only recently had been recognized as an unofficial national holiday, had been promoted since the early twenties by a consortium of florists and conservative political leaders. At a time when publicizing contraception and performing abortion were illegal, despite women's groups of all parties fighting for the legalization of abortion,[14] the establishment of Mother's Day was seen as a backlash against the perpetuation of a more independent New Woman identity.[15] Within this charged political scene, the ringl + pit Mother's Day photograph is not (nor was it intended to be) an overt protest; it merely holds back from extreme sentimentalizing.

This raises the issue of how ringl + pit's work was received at the time and what the effect was of their more critical photographs such as *Petrole Hahn* and *Fragment of a Bride*. The reception of their work can be gauged by sales and by contemporary criticism of ringl + pit's photography. Studio ringl + pit had limited commercial success. It only achieved a small profit in the year before 1933, the year Hitler came to power and the year when Auerbach and Stern emigrated. This lack of financial success can be attributed to both their advertising style and their business disinterest. Although they worked through an agent, they did not usually tailor their work to be sold. For example, they did not retouch their work, and they forbade magazines to alter their photographs. Their work was not bought by the top circulation periodicals; instead it appeared in smaller magazines such as *Neue Frauenkleidung und Frauenkultur* and individual advertising brochures. Within the entire advertising system then, ringl + pit's work had a relatively limited circulation and effect.

Auerbach and Stern did receive positive response from other graphic artists and the avant-garde, however. In this sense, Foto ringl + pit was recognized widely enough to warrant coverage in *Gebrauchsgraphik* (Feb. 1931) and later *Cahiers d'Art* (1934). The bias of *Gebrauchsgraphik* was to promote straight photography in advertising and fight against the far more common pictorialist or heavily retouched style. In both magazines, ringl + pit is represented mainly by its most conventional but formally well-composed still lifes, which glorify the textures and forms of industrial products (for example, the shining wrapper in the 1930 *Gülderning* cigarette ad and the sensual undulations of their close-up textile photography such as *Rayon "Maratti,"* 1931). As photographers, Auerbach and Stern are described in both cases as concerned only with formal matters (emphasized to prove their artistic integrity). *Gebrauchsgraphik* dismisses even their critical humor, stating, "They only like their bit of fun now and then, as when they photograph a bit of stuff and label it 'Fragment of a Bride.'" And, in the following sentence, the author hastens to define ringl + pit's photographs as properly feminine: "They have the inborn womanly instinct for the delicate nuances of textiles, and treat a bale of velvet, a bit of striped flannel or a spool of sewing silk with tireless and self-sacrificial

Ellen Auerbach, *Ringl, Sad,* a portrait of Grete Stern, photograph, 1929. © ringl + pit. Courtesy of the Robert Miller
Gallery, New York.
**(4.6)**

affection until the thing delivers up its soul to make their picture."[16]
Official interpretation of their work was formalist, and ringl + pit's more
critical position was ignored. This tendency continues today. In group
exhibitions of New Vision photography, Stern and Auerbach are often
shown with Peterhans and others as a group concerned only with texture, form, and technical proficiency.

In the end, although ringl + pit's advertising photographs, particularly its image of women, marked a significant critical rejoinder to the conventions of women-as-commodity advertising, the studio did not really intervene markedly or effect change in the context of the German advertising system as a whole. Although *Petrole Hahn* and other ads were published, they hardly disrupted advertising's smooth flow. Overall, the image repertoire of advertising is dependent on economic conditions; advertising is produced by the intersection of several social institutions such as industry and mass media. Therefore systemic changes cannot be caused by single images, particularly given the overdetermined system of representation in advertising. The implicitly critical representations of women developed by Auerbach and Stern can be celebrated within these

Grete Stern, *Pit with Veil,* a portrait of Ellen Auerbach, photograph, 1931. © ringl + pit. Courtesy of the Robert Miller Gallery, New York.
(**4.7**)

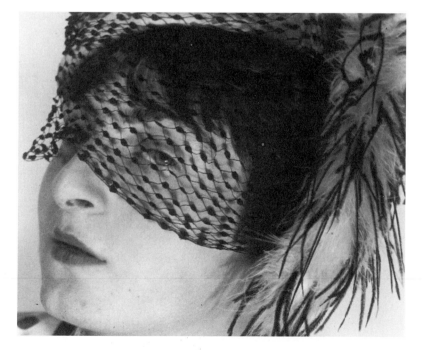

parameters, but with the recognition that these images are perhaps most significant as exceptions. Within the dominant discourse, the differences between ringl + pit's photographs and other contemporary German advertisements are useful in that they clarify the pervasive ideologies and point to alternatives (figs. 4.6, 4.7).

**Notes**

1. Ullrich E. Meisel, "Ein Magazine auf dem Kriegspfad," *Gebrauchsgraphik* 9, Heft 12 (Dec. 1932): 52–53. For example, late twenties and early thirties German advertisements for cameras invariably show women using the photographic equipment. This strategy is evident not only in the women's magazine *Die Dame*, the German equivalent of *Vogue*, but also in the top-circulation newsweekly *Berliner Illustrirte Zeitung* aimed at both male and female readers.

2. In the history of American advertising, see Sally Stein, "The Composite Photographic Image and the Composition of Consumer Ideology," *Art Journal* 41, no. 1 (Spring 1981): 39–45.

3. Atina Grossmann, "The New Woman and the Rationalization of Sexuality in Weimar Germany," in *Powers of Desire: The Politics of Sexuality*, ed. Ann Snitow, Christine Stansell, and Sharon Thompson (New York: Monthly Review Press, 1983), 156–157.

4. On photography and fetishism, see Victor Burgin, "Photography, Phantasy, Function," in his collection *Thinking Photography* (London: Prometheus Books, 1982).

5. *Die Dame* 57, Heft 16 (May 1930): 49.

6. *Berliner Illustrirte Zeitung* 38, no. 29 (July 21, 1929): 1314.

7. Eberhard Holscher, "Photograph Finsler," trans. E.T. Scheffauer, *Gebrauchsgraphik* 8, Heft 4 (April 1931): 7, 9.

8. Politically, neither was active, but they were associated with members of the Redekommunisten, which included Walter Auerbach and Karl Korsch. The Redekommunisten were not part of the German Communist Party (KPD).

9. *Die Dame* 58, Heft 20 (June 1931): 31.

10. Mary Ann Doane, "Film and the Masquerade: Theorising the Female Spectator," *Screen* (Fall 1982): 76–82.

11. Ellen Auerbach, interview with Maud Lavin, April 16, 1985.

12. Joan Riviere, "Womanliness as a Masquerade," in *Psychoanalysis and Female Sexuality*, ed. Hendrik M. Ruitenbeek (New Haven: College and University Press, 1966), 210, 233.

13. Ringl + pit acquired clients through an agent, a man probably from the Mauritius agency. He also made requests from them for generic photographs like *Soap* (1930), which could be sold to a variety of clients and used in different contexts. These requests such as one for more photonarratives were often not to Auerbach's and Stern's liking. Clients' orders would come with stipulations; for example, Rotbart asked that its name be visible and its shaving cream lather look foamy. *Petrole Hahn* was a commis-

sioned photograph and the composition was in part a reaction to the "dopey bottle" and the assignment of promoting it (Ellen Auerbach, interview with M. L., April 16, 1985).

14. Atina Grossmann, "Abortion and Economic Crisis: The 1931 Campaign Against Paragraph 218," in *When Biology Became Destiny: Women in Weimar and Nazi Germany,* ed. Renate Bridenthal, Atina Grossmann, and Marion Kaplan (New York: Monthly Review Press, 1984), 66–86.

15. Karin Hausen, "Mother's Day in the Weimar Republik," in *When Biology Became Destiny,* 131–152.

16. Traugott Schalcher, "Fotostudien Ringl + Pit," trans. E. T. Scheffauer, *Gebrauchsgraphik* 8, Heft 2 (Feb. 1931): 35.

ringl + pit

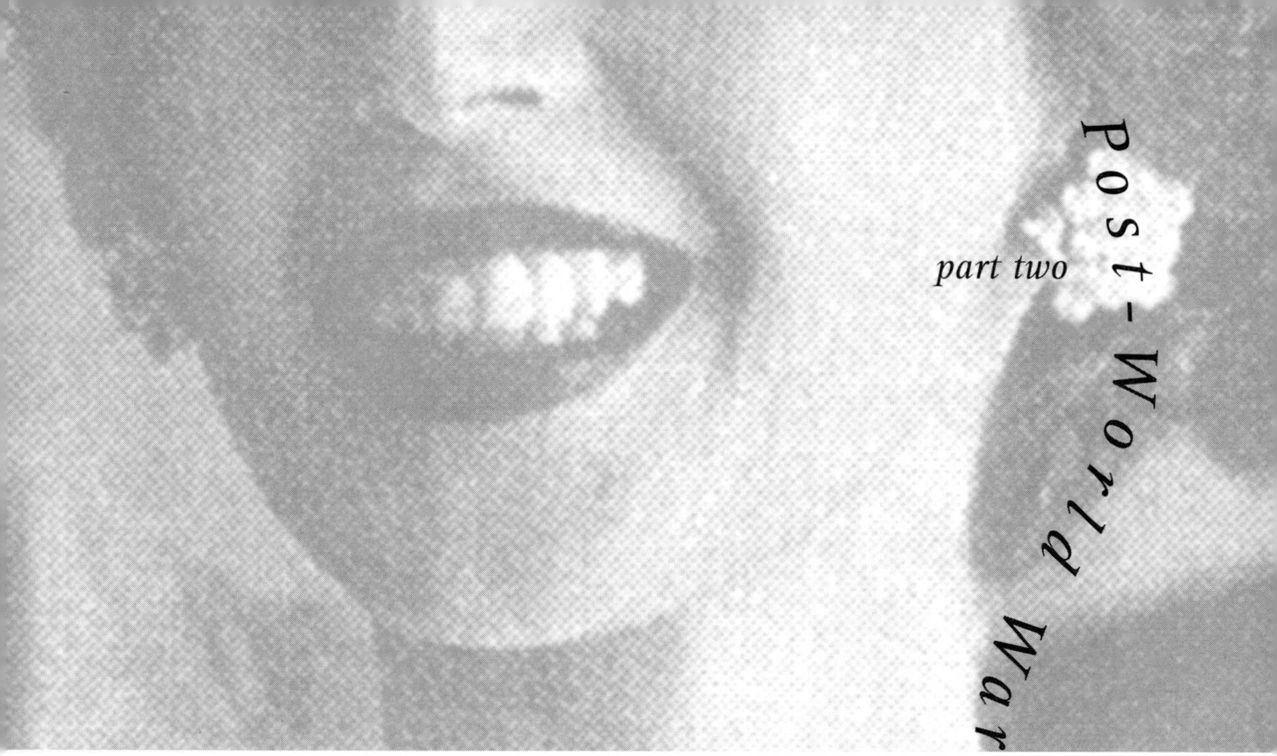

*part two*

# Post-World War II and Today

# U.S. Design in the Service of Commerce—and Alternatives

In the 1980s, General Electric did not striate its trademark. The design logic that gave Prudential's symbol the look of universal cost-code bars and abstracted other company logos out of recognition was less evident with GE. In fact, despite the 1988 implementation of its new global-scale corporate identity program—researched and designed by Landor Associates from 1986 to 1988—General Electric essentially retained its original logo (fig. 5.1). Citing the universal recognizability of the corporation's trademark monogram, Landor recommended altering only a few curlicues. What the designers did change was the trademark's "visual environment," that is, the graphics surrounding it. This decision was in keeping with the traditional evolution of corporate identity programs; following the lead of IBM (and other precursors, such as Olivetti and the Container Corporation of America), multinationals have sought to control their environment visually in order to communicate omniscience and stability.[1] But while this control has come to be standard practice, GE's new identity program has expertly refined a particular psychological aspect of the corporate design challenge: it linked the corporation's look of being all-encompassing to a celebration of the corporation as an individual.

In general, the 1980s were a period during which advertising and design increasingly promoted corporations (and products as their stand-ins) as sanctified individuals. Such promotion entailed more than simply giving a company a personality: it involved ascribing to

5

the company a hyper-individualism, a supremacy as an individual above society. Some dictionary definitions of individualism already conflate personal conduct with economic theory; the word has come to denote both "the leading of one's life in one's own way without regard for others," and laissez-faire economics, "the doctrine that individual freedom in economic enterprise should not be restricted by governmental or social regulation."[2] With the increased implementation of corporate identity programs, advertising and design in the service of commerce have become more explicit and skilled in practicing this conflation. How is this picture of the corporation as an idealized individual conveyed? How has it evolved? How has it affected the design profession, and how have certain designers tried to work outside its framework to address other social issues?

In advertising, a range of visual strategies has been used to personify the corporation. We can see the skilled application of one such strategy by looking more closely at the Landor/GE logo. What is innovative about it is that GE has employed design not only to mark the company as an individual but also to identify that individual as the father. It can be broadly argued that any time authority and regulation are transmitted through the use of a proper name, what is invoked is the name of the father; in this sense, most corporate names and logos can be classified as paternalistic. In the particular case of GE, however, the entire visual environment was mobilized to enhance this kind of paternalism.

Landor Associates, *General Electric logo,* 1986–88. Creative director: Tom Suiter; project director: Don Bartles; designers: Karl Martens, Rebecca Oliver, Randall Dowd, Virginia Zimmerman.
(5.1)

**U.S. Design in the Service of Commerce—and Alternatives**

The visual sign of this fatherly feeling, in GE/Landor language, was called the "dynamic monogram" (fig. 5.2). Accompanying the familiar round and self-enclosed logo was a projection of that same logo, enlarged so greatly that either one-quarter or three-quarters of the sign—depending on which version the given vendor wanted to use—was visible; the rest bled off the edges. The dynamic monogram could not be contained by borders; it looked like a shadow thrown by a giant GE logo looming outside the frame. The design was consistently used on packaging, trucks, ads, signage, and stationery, creating oversized graphic fragments that implicitly place the viewer in the position of a child. In both its size and ubiquity this projection of the logo connoted the role of the archetypal father, promising safety and protection through the authority of his name. The Landor design was an especially felicitous one for the promotion of GE's consumer goods, home appliances, medical technology, and aerospace industries, since domesticity and technology are spheres in which paternalism was traditionally deemed acceptable. The symbolism of Landor's dynamic monogram fit neatly into the con-

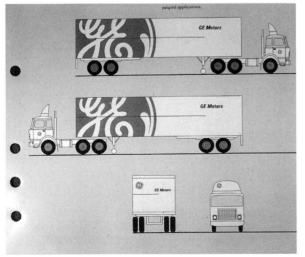

Landor Associates, *GE logo*, dynamic monogram on truck, 1986–88.

**(5.2)**

current BBDO (Batten, Barton, Durstine and Osborn Worldwide, Inc.) ad campaign, particularly the slogan characterizing GE as procreator: "We bring good things to living. We bring good things to life."

In tracing the development of the kind of corporate identity that the GE logo represents, we can begin by asking a large question: How have graphic design and advertising treated issues—either explicitly or implicitly—related to the individualism that is an integral part of American culture? In answering this question we can separate the intention of the designers from the reception of the audience and grant that advertising is not necessarily received in the spirit it is pitched. In fact, the sociologist Michael Schudson has argued that the opposite is true, that advertising fails to persuade the American public. Instead, he claims, advertisers merely follow and encourage existing buying trends.[3] Additionally, we can recognize that advertising is not able to simply celebrate individualism. For its primary task, the promotion of products on a mass scale, is not always congruent with the promotion of individualism.

What's more, tension between the individual and a mass of people has been inherent in much of twentieth-century advertising. Ads are pitched to individual consumers with the implication that the product will make each buyer better and special. At the same time, ads must reach as many people as possible and exhort them to act in an identical way—namely, to buy the product. So, inevitably, no matter what ads say, they promote a certain sameness. Still, acting the same is different from acting in concert, and advertising has long been and can still be criticized for promoting self-centered behavior as opposed to cooperative action.

In order to explore the methods and messages designers use to connect corporate interests with those of society and the individual, a few historical markers are needed. We can see the evolution of how corporate individualism has been represented in American advertising during this century by looking at changes among (1) the 1930s, during which the grim effects of the 1929 stock market crash took hold, ending what had been a period of unparalleled economic growth and consumer purchasing power; (2) the 1950s, characterized by the buying sprees of postwar prosperity, conformism in the interest of business and country, and labor

Designer unknown, *Advertisement for the United Hotels Company of America, Fortune* (Feb. 1930): 15.
(5.3)

unrest; and (3) the 1980s, a period of conservative, pro-business government during which the identities and images of United States–based
multinational corporations were solidified in the face of serious international threats to American economic dominance.

In his book *Captains of Consciousness*, the sociologist and historian Stuart
Ewen finds that advertising functioned as early as the 1920s to aid "the
business community . . . setting up itself, or its personified corporate self,
as a model for emulation. . . . The authority of industry was being drawn
as a sustaining *father* figure while the traditional arenas of social inter-
course and the possibility of collective action were pictured as decrepit,
threatening and basically incapable of providing any level of security."[4]
Similarly, the cultural critic Raymond Williams accuses advertising of promoting an individualistic turn away from communal action.[5] Yet the historian Roland Marchand, in his survey of American advertising from
1920 to 1940, finds that advertising during that period addressed anxieties produced by modernization and shows that the preaching of consumerism functioned not only to sell products but also to repersonalize
American life. By building bridges between individual consumer actions
and mass appeal, he argues, advertising served to finess the differences
between local and national scales inherent in modernization.[6]

In fact, when surveying print ads of the 1920s and early 1930s, we
can often find a dual appeal to the individual and to the community. In
some instances, as in an ad that appeared in *Fortune* magazine in 1930, the
idea of community is directly tied to the corporation—the corporation
being a substitute for other forms of community (fig. 5.3). In this ad for
United Hotels, the organization of the hotel chain is likened to that of
large-scale steel and automobile companies. Graphics and copy combine
to summon up the image of the chain as the community of the future.
The drawing shows cubes of city buildings towering upward, illuminated
by beams of light, with modern block type breaking in from below. The
headline, which must have held appeal in light of the recent stock market
crash, reads: "United Fortunes." The ad copy promises "centralized control and supervision" and also inspired service by individuals, which, it
claims, cannot be standardized.[7] In such ways, advertising during the

## "...and I'll live like a princess in a house that runs like magic..."

"I have a wonderful post-war dream . . .

"I'm always fresh as a daisy, pretty as a picture . . . and housekeeping — in my new all-Gas home of the future — seems like play!

"I work in a kitchen that's cool, clean, free from cooking odors . . . where, with no trouble at all, I turn out dishes that make my family want to hug me. For my new Certified Performance Gas range is amazingly efficient — with heat controls so accurate they cut out all sorts of work and watching . . . save food values and cooking time!

"I open my magic Gas refrigerator . . . my silent storeroom . . . and what do I see? . . . All kinds of foods, meats, vegetables, even frozen foods . . . Yes, special cooling units keep them fresh longer,

save hours of marketing time.

"I turn on my permanent 'hot springs' . . . and an automatic Gas water-heating system gives me oceans of hot water whenever I want it.

"Why, even the weather is mine for the asking . . . for my new Gas air-conditioning system gives me luxurious warmth in January, mountain coolness in July!"

Dream on, lady . . . For tomorrow these and other miracles of comfort will be brought to you by the tiny blue Gas flame . . . *the flame that cools as well as heats.* You can speed that day by using Gas wisely . . . and by saving for your home of the future with every War Bond you can buy.

*THE MAGIC FLAME THAT WILL BRIGHTEN YOUR FUTURE*

AMERICAN GAS ASSOCIATION **GAS**

Designer unknown, *Advertisement for the American Gas Association, House & Garden* (May 1944): 18.
**(5.4)**

Great Depression alluded to frictions among the individual, the community, and the corporation. Yet what is troubling about the United ad is its suggestion that the whole range of issues surrounding the identity of an individual in a community can be resolved within a framework that relates the individual exclusively to the corporation.

The appeal to community that we see in some depression-era ads gives way to a focus on individual experience in ads from the World War II years and the 1950s. Postwar economic prosperity initiated a surge in buying and created a desire to build a new world rooted in the private family dwelling. A full-page ad in the May 1944 issue of *House & Garden* anticipates the coming of this climate (fig. 5.4).[8] At the top of the page is an image of a woman lying in a bubble bath who wears a crown and is surrounded by angels. Below we see the same woman, hanging up clothes with the help of her husband outside their single-family house. The heading, "and I'll live like a princess in a house that runs like magic," is followed by copy that reads, "I have a wonderful post-war dream . . . I'm always fresh as a daisy, pretty as a picture . . . and housekeeping—in my new all-Gas home of the future—seems like play!"[9]

In ads of the 1950s, identification between the consumer and the product (and therefore the corporation) is stressed. Design of that decade contributed to this emphasis by allowing only a highly simplified, condensed, seemingly essential reading of the message. It was in the same period that the necessity of an equally hard-hitting, unambiguous corporate image was recognized. As *Print* magazine reported in 1959: "The merchant is realizing that unless the prospective customer can consciously or unconsciously see a 'fit' between her own self-image and the image of the store, she will not patronize it, no matter what price offerings are made. It is perfectly logical, therefore, for the manufacturer to inquire whether a similar attraction or repulsion may be taking place between the consuming public and his company's personality which would have bearing on the sale of his products."[10]

Postwar ad design, in contrast to the storyboard and cartoonlike ads of the 1930s, is stark, with large, legible images. This tendency is evident in an ad for Handmacher's women's suits that appeared in a 1954 issue of

WHO
ME?

Yes, *you* in the Handmacher. The most beautiful suit of the season. Look how softly it curves to the figure. How charming in every detail. Ample evidence of the genius of styling and mastery of tailoring that is uniquely Handmacher's. Tailored in Striette woolen. The bib effect is its own perfect linen blouse revealed. Misses and Junior Sizes. $89⁹⁵

TAILORED BY

*handmacher* ® "YOU CAN FEEL THE GOOD FIT"

WRITE TO DEPT. V-2, HANDMACHER-VOGEL, INC., 501 SEVENTH AVENUE, NEW YORK 18

Designer unknown, *Advertisement for Handmacher, Vogue*
(Feb. 1, 1954): 32.
(**5.5**)

*Vogue* magazine; the photo fills five-sixths of the page (fig. 5.5). A woman in a suit stands with three men in business suits. She points to herself, and the type next to her reads: "Who me?" The copy answers: "Yes, *you* in the Handmacher. The most beautiful suit of the season." Her identity and ability to be distinguished from men. ("Look how softly it curves to the figure") are attributed wholly to the product.[11]

The 1980s brought a diversification of advertising approaches such as event advertising and micromarketing. Nevertheless, in general, it is easy to see a continuation of the advertising trend to represent individual experience as if completely contained within an environment defined by corporation, brand name, and product. In the characteristic ad of the 1980s, the consumer exists through the product, and the product is author of a lifestyle; that is, the product takes the place of the person within American myths of individualism. (Which is not to say that prospective buyers were necessarily brainwashed by this message, for consumers during this decade voiced vigorous skepticism about advertising while at the same time acknowledging their delight in its high production values.) If one ad could be said to be exemplary of the 1980s "you-*are*-the-product" (as compared with the 1950s "you-*are*-*identified*-with-the-product") trend, it is the first Michelob beer TV commercial in "The Night Belongs to Michelob" series, which aired in 1986. The entire sixty-second spot is a sequence of dark liquid and night-light shots, all of which dissolve to approximate a look of gleaming fluidity. This is not a narrative but a montage of the coolness, wetness, camaraderie, and sexuality available in the proffered night. The beer personifies the night, and the ad suggests that the viewer can attain this nocturnal experience not just by consuming Michelob but by becoming Michelob.

Where does design fit into this framework of advertising, individualism, and the corporation? What is its function, and does it have any power to change an ad's message, to reflect the interaction between the individual and society or between the individual and the community? Does design, within the limits of corporate advertising, have the power to raise questions about the notion of the corporation as an individual? The skeptical answer to these questions is no. Design in the service of com-

U.S. Design in the Service of Commerce—and Alternatives

merce is subordinate, after all, to the desires of its clients as well as to the canons of the design profession, which typically emphasize "simplicity," "honesty," "legibility," and "abbreviation." Some postwar designers reacted to these restrictions by employing wit and humor and by pursuing formal innovation; The Pushpin Group and Dan Friedman immediately come to mind. Nineties advertising was often heavily ironic. But are formal innovations or irony really able to effect substantial change in the message communicated?

The argument can be made that, in graphic design, formal innovation in and of itself is not so important as the selection and juxtaposition of signifying fragments. For design is montage, a recycling of common symbols in new combinations and visual environments. It is precisely because design recirculates easily understood and shared imagery—and is widely distributed—that it is so powerful. Given this immense ability to communicate, the challenge to graphic designers is to focus less exclusively on formal concerns and more on the context and content of the message. While designers are by definition dependent on clients, they can choose clients, corporate and nonprofit, in such a way as to increase their involvement in the shaping of messages.

What does this selectivity mean in specific cases? Consider a comparison of Paul Rand's work with that done by William Golden during the 1950s. The two men shared attitudes toward design and even much visual vocabulary, although Rand more clearly embraced certain visual standards established by avant-garde art. Despite these parallels, some of Golden's designs for CBS and Rand's for IBM evince quite distinct philosophical differences.

In his writings, Rand talks of simplicity, repetition, striation, letters, and brevity, and he designs accordingly; his logos for ABC (1962) and IBM (1956) are cases in point. Perhaps Rand's noncorporate work is formally more provocative, as evidenced by the covers he did during the late 1930s and early 1940s for the antifascist cultural magazine Direction. However, in his corporate identity programs, visual puns are as far as he goes in the direction of complexity. (Recall his rebus for a 1981 IBM poster, in which the "I" is represented by the image of an eye and the "B" by a bee.) Rand believes the designer should pursue simplicity in order to divine some abstract "truth." His argument seems to be that essentialism of form is equivalent to the essence of truth, a common modernist maxim but one that does not bear close scrutiny. If we think in particular about how design represents a multinational corporation such as IBM, Rand's client for decades, it is clear that striated letters do little to reflect the "truth" of this enormous technological, economic, and cultural complex. In his book *Paul Rand: A Designer's Art* he endorses the statement made by Irwin Miller of the Cummins Engine company that "Good design at heart is simply honesty."[12] Variations on this ingenuous claim pass for received wisdom in many design courses and among many working designers; it is a claim that keeps the focus of the profession on visual minutiae and away from the responsibilities that come with its tremendous power to communicate.

There seems to be a shared belief system operating in the case of effectively implemented corporate identity programs. By and large, the design profession has since the 1950s accepted IBM's proposition that "IBM's 'Corporate Image'" can be summed up: good design itself is the image."[13] In the course of praising Rand's fresh and clean IBM logo in 1959, Joe Carty, then the organization's head of advertising and corporate promotions, said, "All we're trying to do is to communicate IBM as a company that is serving in an orderly, efficient and honest manner."[14]

But such deceptively bland credos are of course not the entire basis for this belief system. As the designer Wally Olins points out in his 1978 book *The Corporate Personality,* corporate identity programs were primarily developed after World War II, emerging with the establishment of the huge multinationals and reflecting their desires to monopolize markets globally and to communicate continuity and stability in a variety of cultures. Olins observes that these desires have produced identity programs that seek to make the clients appear "homogeneous," "strong," "cool," "distant," "controlled," "smooth," "unwrinkled," "all-knowing." "ubiquitous," "all-seeing," "ordered," "superhuman," "expensive," "modern," and in charge of nature.[15] "If companies share the idea of corporate omniscience," he contends, "it is inevitable that they will tend to look similar,"

William Golden, drawing by Ben Shahn, *Program advertisement for the CBS program* See It Now, various formats, 1958. (5.6)

William Golden, drawing by Ben Shahn, *Program advertisement for the CBS program* See It Now, various formats, 1957. (5.7)

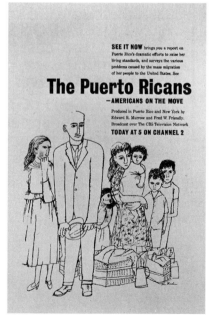

going on to complain that "corporate design is for the most part as stiff, sullen, aggressive and self-glorifying as it was 10 or even 20 years ago."[16]

Given the restrictions of this belief system, and the willingness of most designers to accept them, it is an illuminating contrast to look at the career of William Golden. He worked for CBS radio and television in the 1940s and 1950s and was the television network's creative director of advertising and sales promotion from 1951 until his untimely death in 1959. Golden is well known for designing the CBS trademark, which symbolizes both the viewer's eye and the camera's lens. Outside his corporate work he produced designs for political causes, such as posters for presidential candidate Adlai Stevenson. But even at CBS, Golden, with collaborators such as the leftist artist Ben Shahn, was able to make certain liberal social statements. Take, for example, two newspaper advertisements designed by Golden with artwork by Shahn for Fred Friendly and Edward R. Murrow's *See It Now* documentary series (1951–58). Both feature simple blocks of boldface type and pen-and-ink drawings. Golden laid the drawings out to take up more than half the page, increasing their impact further by not framing them. For a 1958 show on the effects of nuclear fallout, Shahn drew two bald people anxiously looking skyward (fig. 5.6). A similarly humanistic approach is evident in the ad for a 1957 episode of *See It Now* entitled "The Puerto Ricans—Americans on the Move," for which Shahn drew a family of immigrants standing together, looking apprehensive, their belongings gathered around them (fig. 5.7). So, Golden and Shahn were able to editorialize, due to their unusual corporate context and the liberal self-image CBS News had during the early days of television. Today the corporate design climate is altogether more rigid.

In his writings Golden shares Paul Rand's adulation of order, simplicity, and legibility. Yet unlike Rand he does not conflate these formal issues with the communication of a mythic essential truth. Moreover, Golden is skeptical about the function of design in the service of commerce: "For Business wants him [the designer] to help create an attitude about the facts, not to communicate them. And only about some of the facts. For facts in certain juxtapositions can offend some portion of the market. So he finds himself working with half-truths, and feels that he is not using all his talents. He finds that he is part of a giant merchandising apparatus in which the media of mass communication have reached a miraculous degree of technical perfection and are being operated at full speed to say as little as necessary in the most impressive way."[17]

Designers face constraints in the service of commerce. Even when a given corporation allows a graphic designer to comment on broad social issues, the designer, quite naturally, will not be able to communicate insights about the operation of the corporation or its relationship to the economy and society. Instead, by focusing exclusively on the corporation, design in this context contributes to a celebration of the organization as a supreme individual in society. And yet, while graphic design as a field is dependent upon funding and clients, it need not be entirely reliant on corporations.

Given that corporate design is virtually closed to the more critical varieties of social commentary, graphic designers who wish to address social issues in their work—and to have that work widely disseminated—tend to choose between two alternatives: liberal pro bono work, generally done for public-service groups and well-funded socially oriented organizations; and more politically radical work, addressing systemic issues, which typically relies on a variety of marginal sources for funding. The latter designs treat subjects ranging from sexism and racism to international trade and the environment. Besides dealing with social questions, both types of work can also raise questions about how graphic design produces meaning formally, for example, counteracting the prevalent essentialism-above-all ethos through such techniques as layering and montage.

Free or low-paid pro bono work is done by small and large design firms alike seeking both to do public service and to receive recognition. Most of these firms feel they cannot afford to alienate anyone and so stick to safe subjects. Landor Associates, for instance, is aggressive in pursuing blue-chip pro bono projects, and in the past has lent a helping hand to such needy clients as the America's Cup, the Nobel Foundation, and Prince Philip. These designs most frequently take the form of logos and letterheads. Still, there are many creative designs done for less glamorous and more broad-based causes, such as Ken Diamond's graphics for the New York State branch of Planned Parenthood and his brochures for the Bureau of Waste Prevention's recycling efforts in Brooklyn. (Diamond does not do this work for free; instead he has a lower rate for nonprofit organizations.) In university and community settings, Sheila Levrant de Bretteville has produced activist graphics, for example, on working-class history. For community politics, Qris Yamashita creates posters for Asian Pacific and Japanese American causes such as Los Angeles's annual Day of Remembrance, marking the memory of Japanese American internments during World War II.

Graphic design, with its inherent ability to communicate broadly through a recycling and reordering of our common visual vocabulary, is ideally suited to address larger problems and societal change. Such projects, though, whether circumscribed or unfettered, are hard to fund. However, a number of designers have independently managed to produce effective activist work, conceived of according to the urgency of issues rather than the demands of clients. Facilitating this work is the fact that design technology has become increasingly accessible through computers; small groups and individuals now approach large issues via a cottage-industry route. But if high-quality production has gotten easier, reaching a large public has gotten more difficult.

In conclusion, I want to look at two designers working in a cottage-industry way who have developed an editorial or opinionated voice in a public forum. The first is Stephen Kroninger who can also be described as a photomontage artist and an illustrator. Starting in the early eighties to publish in such "alternative" venues as *The Progressive* (Madison) and *The Village Voice* (New York), Kroninger has now become an authorial name, and he is assigned covers for *Time* and work for other national publications such as *Newsweek*, *Esquire*, and *Entertainment Weekly*. Amazingly enough in this time of monopolization and centralization of the media, which has meant a flattening of individual voices, Kroninger is able to retain a strong personal voice of political caricature.

Kroninger's style is purposefully crude. The lettering, for example, in his *The President consults his top foreign policy advisor: Popular opinion* (1994, for *The*

*Village Voice*) is uneven, cut from different magazines, the stuff of poison pen letters (fig. 5.8). Typically, Kroninger distills from media reporting, as in his *Japan buys a used president* (Nov. 4, 1989, for *The New York Times*) commenting on Reagan's highly paid trip to Japan. Kroninger lifts a direct quote from President Bush in his *The most qualified man in America! Who's fantasizing?*, criticizing Bush's nomination of Clarence Thomas for the Supreme Court. But he also comments on the media—when we see Clinton staring at opinion poll results on the television, it reminds us of the foggy media habit of covering U.S. foreign policy in terms of its popularity at home instead of its actual impact in the relevant foreign country and on U.S. national security.

Privately owned newspapers and magazines are not required to operate as public forums and to give voice to private opinions other than those of their owners. Legally, though, public spaces, or forums affiliated with the government, are democratically open to a kaleidoscope of ideas that in turn are protected by First Amendment rights of freedom of speech. But what about spaces like shopping malls, subway cars, bus advertisement spaces, and billboards in train stations? Are these public or

Stephen Kroninger, *The President consults his top foreign policy advisor: Popular opinion*, photomontage for *The Village Voice*, 1994.
**(5.8)**

private? Who has the right to speak there? Artist and designer Michael Lebrón, with money earned from his day job as art director for pharmaceutical advertisements, has been buying ad space in subway cars in New York City and Washington, D.C., and in the Amtrak train area of New York's Penn Station. These he fills with his political graphics, which combine political caricature and calls for direct action into the spaces. With his montages, Lebrón has protested the Reagan administration's policy on the homeless and public housing and urged a boycott of Coors beer for the Coors family's involvement with the Nicaraguan contras. Three times he's gone to court when the powers that be have balked upon seeing his content and tried to censor him. Each time he's won, cheerful news for him and landmark news for anyone who wants to participate in public debate in places that are increasingly privatized. His 1993–95 fight with Amtrak went all the way to the Supreme Court where Lebrón was represented by David Cole of The Center for Constitutional Rights. Lebrón won that case, significantly proving that Amtrak, although private, was heavily subsidized and managed by the government, and therefore owed citizens the cacophonous rights to a "public" space. In fact, the decision extends beyond the First Amendment to other civil rights as well. As Justice Antonin Scalia summarized in his opinion, the "government, state or federal, . . . [cannot] . . . evade the most solemn obligations imposed in the Constitution by simply resorting to the corporate form." Whether through the extensive newspaper coverage of Lebrón's court battles or the publicly placed graphics themselves, Lebrón has been effective in reaching, stirring, and serving a broad audience.

Unfortunately, the funding and audience situations of designers like Ken Diamond, Sheila Levrant de Bretteville, Stephen Kroninger, Qris Yamashita, and Michael Lebrón are the exceptions not the rule. The rule in the design profession is work for corporate hire. The ever-increasing tendency of corporations, beginning in the 1920s, to use graphic design to promote their products and enhance their images, and the postwar belief that even small businesses should look "modern" or "designed," have provided much-needed livelihood for the design profession, but at the same time combined to work against it in other ways. The growing popularity of design within the business community has led the profession to see itself as chiefly client-oriented. The accepted function of the designer has become one of providing a service rather than generating ideas to be communicated; this self-definition discourages explicitly political expression. However, possibilities exist for those who want to imaginatively pursue activist and/or personal design projects that are alternatives to working for businesses and large organizations. These expressive projects can also supplement corporate design, and the multi-tasking work of entrepreneurial design firms like ReVerb in Los Angeles and studio blue and Thirst in Chicago are hopeful models. Beyond this, the challenge to the profession as a whole is to redefine the societal role of the designer in a way that more broadly engages the mass-communicative powers of graphic design.

## Notes

1. Adrian Forty, *Objects of Desire: Design and Society from Wedgwood to IBM* (New York: Pantheon Books, 1986).

2. *Webster's New World Dictionary of the American Language* (Cleveland: World Publishing Company, 1966), 743.

3. Michael Schudson, *Advertising: The Uneasy Persuasion* (New York: Basic Books, 1984).

4. Stuart Ewen, *Captains of Consciousness: Advertising and the Roots of Consumer Culture* (New York: McGraw-Hill, 1976), 102.

5. Raymond Williams, "The Magic System," in *Problems in Materialism and Culture* (London: Verso, 1980), 170–195.

6. Roland Marchand, *Advertising the American Dream: Making Way for Modernity, 1920–1940* (Berkeley: University of California Press, 1985).

7. *Fortune* 1, no. 1 (February 1930): 15.

8. See Dolores Hayden, *Redesigning the American Dream: The Future of Housing, Work, and Family Life* (New York: W. W. Norton, 1984); and Roland Marchand, "Visions of Classlessness, Quests for Dominion: American Popular Culture, 1945–1960," in *Reshaping America: Society and Institutions, 1945–1960,* ed. Robert H. Brenner and Gary M. Reichard (Columbus: Ohio State University Press, 1982), 163–192.

9. *House & Garden* 85 (May 1944): 18.

10. Pierre Martineau, "Sharper Focus for the Corporate Image," *Print* 13, no. 3 (May–June 1959): 22. The designers Lou Dorfsman and Herb Lubalin served as guest editors of this issue, which was devoted to the corporate image.

11. *Vogue* 123 (1 Feb. 1954): 32.

12. *Paul Rand: A Designer's Art* (New Haven: Yale University Press, 1985). The statement was made in a talk given by Miller, then chairman of Cummins's executive committee, on June 14, 1984, after his company had received a design award from the American Institute of Graphic Arts.

13. "IBM's 'New Look,'" Print 13, no. 3 (May–June 1959): 25.

14. Quoted in "IBM's 'New Look,'" Print 13, no. 3 (May–June 1959): 25.

15. Wally Olins, *The Corporate Personality: An Inquiry into the Nature of Corporate Identity* (London: Design Council, 1978).

16. Olins, *The Corporate Personality*, 77.

17. Cipe Pineles Golden, Kurt Weihs, and Robert Strunsky, ed., *The Visual Craft of William Golden* (New York: George Braziller, 1962), 61. For a different yet related comparison of Rand and Golden, see Lorraine Wild, "Art and Design: Lovers or Just Good Friends," *AIGA Journal of Graphic Design* 5, no. 2 (1987): 2–3.

# New Traditionalism and Corporate Identity

During the 1988 presidential campaign, Bob Dole dismissed George Bush as "nothing but a suit." This was an apt indictment. It identified Bush with the fuddy-duddy dad of *Father Knows Best* and the ultimate gray-flannel company man. Although Dole's comment was meant as a denunciation, it contained the recognition as well of Bush's uncanny ability to reawaken the stylish mediocrity of the 1950s.

Shortly after Bush's inauguration as president in January 1989, *Good Housekeeping* coined the term "New Traditionalism" for a series of ads that offered New Traditionalism its domestic representation—WASPy moms choosing, once again, to stay home with the kids. This was followed by increased advertising for brands that had been around since the 1950s but were now aggressively revivified—Kool Aid, Corn Flakes, Geritol. In just six months, the term "New Traditionalism" and the advertising campaigns it spawned became pervasive, promoting a backward-looking consumer utopia, a return to the conventions of the nuclear family, and a fifties-style allegiance to patriarchy and patriotism. After so many news photographs of Barbara walking the dog and George playing horseshoes, Americans came to recognize the Bush family as New Traditionalists—and an unsubtle and unusually tightly fitted congruence between presidential image and corporate identity.

In design terms, corporate identity programs establish a "look," not only through advertising, but in packaging, logos, letterheads, and graphics. As much of the

6

public personality of the company as can be presented is coordinated visually. In the late 1980s, a shift in design strategy for constructing corporate identity occurred, a movement away from the futuristic and toward the traditional. In these designs, what was "traditional" was generally an ersatz affirmation of the good old days, an arm's reach back to postwar prosperity, yet curiously updated. Take two late 1980s examples of New Traditionalism in corporate identity. In 1988 the huge multinational conglomerate IC Industries, maker of, among other products, Progresso Italian Foods, Midas mufflers, and Hussmann refrigerator equipment, decided its name was too severe. So IC simply appropriated the name of one of its homier brands, the chocolate manufacturer Whitman, and renamed itself Whitman Corp. What could be more reassuring than chocolate? In another instance, Prudential Life Insurance, swept up in an earlier craze for futuristic logos—a trend linked to the high-tech, anonymous, hardball corporate images of the pre-crash 1980s—had turned its familiar Rock of Gibraltar logo into something that looked like a broken price code bar. But by early 1989, Prudential—whose stake as an insurance company in the cradling message of New Traditionalist-style stability was great—had dropped the striations from its rock and returned to a simpler, realistic, and more recognizable line drawing of Gibraltar (fig. 6.1). This cultural tendency, though, was more than just a design trend: new consensuses were being formulated and underlined by New Traditionalist visuals. The man in the suit was firmly back in power, and low-key, well-executed design invited us once again to feel comfortable with (or at least uncritical of) this idea.

Beyond the subtleties of corporate logo styles, fear of the future was soothed most visibly in advertising campaigns. New Traditionalist ads asked the viewer to compare today with yesterday and tomorrow: they raised anxiety about what was next; and then they gave conservative, *gently conservative* answers: "you'll be the same in the future, but don't worry, you won't be outmoded." Perhaps the ultimate New Traditionalist ad campaign was the TV one for the Mazda Miata car. (The name "Miata" itself was a clever marketing montage; it contained that most consumerist word "me" and it sounded like some new 1989 Esperanto that combined

New Traditionalism and Corporate Identity

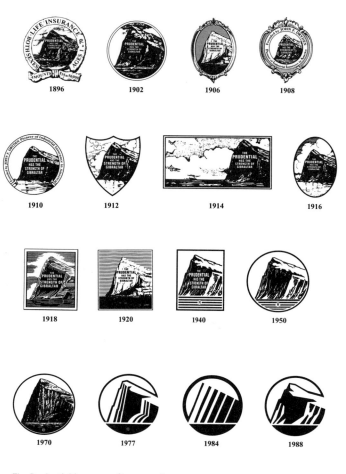

*Rock of Gibraltar logos,* The Prudential Insurance Company of
America, 1896–1988. Reprinted with the permission of The
Prudential Company of America. All rights reserved.
(6.1)

the languages of Japan and the United States). There were two thirty-sec-
ond spots: the Miata in the city and the Miata in the country. In the country ad, the camera panned across well-off suburban kids playing on their
lawns—the light was too bright, it looked slightly eerie, the voiceover
used past tense. Was this the future or the past? A thirtyish man was

shown confusingly with a fifties haircut and brand-new blue jeans. Eventually we saw the bright red car. The tag line was perfect: "It not only gives you a glimpse of 1990, it takes you back as well." The final image was the nuclear suburban family relaxing on a day in the country. The image of the family underlined the retiring nature of these utopias—even the city ad, which showed the requisite skyscrapers and cars on city streets, included a shot of a wedding.

These New Traditionalist utopian images were radically different from more liberatory scenes, ones in which risks, change, and new pleasures could be imagined. The deeply conservative nature of backward-looking utopias has been theorized before, not surprisingly, by Ernst Bloch, a writer who explored why the Right had become so popular in the years immediately preceding Nazi Germany. In the early 1930s, writing about German culture as a political battlefield, Bloch pointed out that the desire for such anachronistic utopias can be rooted in fear and can circumvent more constructive fantasies of change. At the same time, he emphasized the lure of cultural messages mixing anachronistic and contemporary visions. This kind of mix was the bait of New Traditionalism in corporate identity programs: New Traditionalist ads and graphics waylaid fear by promising the isolationism (in 1980s parlance "cocooning") of the 1950s in a familiar yet up-to-date package. Reassuringly, the future was offered as a retooled version of the past. New Traditionalism was not simply traditionalism but an up-to-the-minute revamping, a pastiche in which the old is dominant, merely coated with the new.

In financial terms, the consumer must be convinced that a product has some new qualities as well as old. Otherwise, why purchase it? Specifically, these old/new products were offered as a balm to economic anxieties; ads encouraged consumers to ward off financial worries by shoring up domestic comfort. For baby boomers, stylized old-fashioned corporate graphics were retreads of symbols familiar since childhood and recalled cozy supermarket and kitchen scenes from the fifties. Prompted by names like Bosco, Jiffy, and Jell-O, these memories were reassuring, but they worked too well in sewing corporate power into the same form as the presidential suit.

New Traditionalism and Corporate Identity

# Collectivism in the Decade of Greed:

## Political Art Coalitions in the 1980s in New York City

In 1979, the year twelve artists formed the collective Group Material, no one I knew took Ronald Reagan's bid for the presidency seriously. Even the centrist newspaper of record, *The New York Times*, was watching the early candidacies of George Bush and Howard Baker, not that of right-wing nut (as he was still then widely considered) Reagan. The signs for a national swing rightward were clear, though. Looking back now through the *Times* headlines from 1979 and with the aid of hindsight, it's easy to find many warnings reported: anxiety about the economy and unemployment, scrambling to avert another energy crisis in the future, decline in auto sales and profits of other manufacturing industries, alarm over the hostage situation in Iran. Jimmy Carter was on his way out. And yet, at the same time, the last flickerings of a popular liberalism were visible; the 1979 *Times* also documents that the best-of-hippydom, women's health bible *Our Bodies, Ourselves*, by a feminist collective in Boston, was on the best-seller list and that federal National Endowment for the Arts grants were going increasingly to smaller, grass-roots cultural groups. This was the overarching political environment, then, in which members of Group Material including Julie Ault, Mundy McLaughlin, and Tim Rollins (key participants Doug Ashford and Felix Gonzales-Torres joined later) decided to open a community-based gallery in New York's East Village to address issues of culture and politics. The waning days of seventies liberalism marked

7

Group Material's open and inclusive character and, in general, encouraged the American Left's operative dream that a radical democracy situated even to the left of a status quo liberal model was possible.

As the eighties progressed, though, and the United States endured the "conservative revolution" of two consecutive Reagan terms (1980–84, 1984–88), an expansive outreach position on the Left, one that presented alternative societal models, became almost untenable and/or restricted to extremely small constituencies. There was no liberal mainstream, and many leftist groups, art-based and otherwise, were forced to turn to patching up fast-disappearing social services. A radical vision of reconstructing the United States economically such as Marxism was shoved onto the back shelves of university libraries as even the most basic liberal ideas like funding social services with tax dollars were shredded by a rapacious turn toward pure capitalism. The effects of cutting social services like housing for the indigent and health insurance for the working poor became immediately apparent—although for the most part unprotested—as homeless people filled the streets and minimum wage workers fell into welfare to get health coverage. As many commentators on both the Left and Right have noted, the eighties was the decade when the rich got richer and the poor got poorer.

Yet, the sheer lack of government responsibility, the utter heartlessness of Reagan's hands-off approach, galvanized many artists, design activists, and intellectuals to fill the political void—or at least try to. This was evident across the country although most visible in New York City due to media coverage. Because both the art and print media worlds were so centralized in New York, particularly in this era just before the Internet took hold and loosened geographic cultural clustering, the majority of political art collectives that became most well known and most influential were New York–based. Not all collaborative groups sought to make an impact on everyday U.S. politics and society. Some were fairly traditional cooperations between artists in the marketplace. Others more commonly used techniques of design activism to act in concert as lobbying groups to influence either art world or governmental practices, or both.

Collectivism in the Decade of Greed

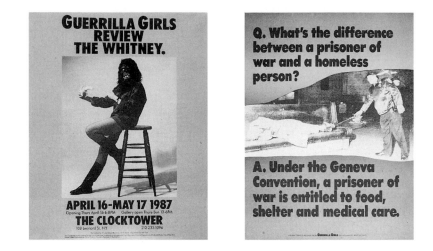

Strategies changed in the eighties for art activists; specifically they used design techniques familiar from newspaper layouts and poster propaganda. Both Guerrilla Girls (founded in 1985) and Gran Fury (formed in 1988) coalesced primarily around single issues: the Guerrilla Girls to fight art-world gender- and race-based exclusions (fig. 7.1), Gran Fury to wage war on AIDS ignorance, intolerance, and inaction. It's not surprising that the activist artists and writers of Weimar Germany like John Heartfield, with their pragmatic, media-savvy approaches to resisting the encroachment of the far Right, became the intellectual heroes of eighties activist art groups in the United States, even at times providing the visual models for these New York City collaboratives.

Much more important, though, to 1980s art activism than looking back to the 1920s was the depletion of urban life quality (for all but the wealthy) under the Reagan and Bush administrations. For the Guerrilla Girls, the prosperity of some white male artists and exclusion of many in the eighties art world paralleled what was going on in the national economy. In the mid-eighties, for example, women in the United States earned on the average 60 cents to the dollar men earned, and two out of three adults living in poverty were female. For impoverished families, sta-

*Opposite left:*
Guerilla Girls, *Guerilla Girls Review the Whitney,* poster, first exhibited at The Clocktower, New York, 1987. "A not-for-profit gallery, The Clocktower, asked us to do a show during the Whitney Museum of American Art's Biennial in 1987. They expected us to do a show of art we thought should be in the biennial. Instead, we decided to do an exhibition of information exposing the museum's pathetic and worsening record on women and artists of color."
(**7.1**)

*Opposite right:*
Guerilla Girls, *What's the difference between a prisoner of war and a homeless person?,* poster, 1991.
(**7.2**)

*Above:*
Gran Fury, *Let the Record Show . . . ,* window installation, The New Museum, New York, 1987.
(**7.3**)

*At left:*
Gran Fury, *Welcome to America,* poster, 1989.
(**7.4**)

Gran Fury, *The Pope and the Penis,* two-part billboard, 1990. This work was first exhibited in the Aperto exhibition that was part of the 1990 Venice Biennale.
   Due to official questioning of the work as blasphemous (papal magistrates eventually declared that it was not), exhibition of the billboards was delayed beyond the opening of the exhibition and the works were allowed on the walls only later.
(**7.5**)

KISSING DOESN'T KILL: GREED AND INDIFFERENCE DO.

CORPORATE GREED, GOVERNMENT INACTION, AND PUBLIC INDIFFERENCE MAKE AIDS A POLITICAL CRISIS.

Gran Fury, *Kissing doesn't kill. Greed and indifference do,*
bus poster, 1989.
**(7.6)**

tistics were worst for black and Latina mothers: 51.7 percent of black
female-headed households were poor as were 53.4 percent of Latina families headed by single women. And once the Guerrilla Girls became firmly established as the self-proclaimed "conscience of the art world," effectively finger-wagging and shaming museums and galleries into slowly
starting to improve representation of women and minorities through
unrelenting nighttime postering of New York City walls (called sniping—
illegally wheat-pasting posters around the city)—they increasingly turned
to highlighting national problems. For example, a 1991 poster showed a
homeless person and read: "Q. What's the difference between a prisoner
of war and a homeless person? A. Under the Geneva Convention, a prisoner of war is entitled to food, shelter and medical care" (fig. 7.2).

Gran Fury came on the scene as a kind of visual arts stepchild of the
political group ACT UP (AIDS Coalition to Unleash Power). ACT UP was
founded primarily by gay charter members in 1987, the year Republican
Senator Jesse Helms pushed through federal legislation refusing government funds for any educational materials that depict or condone homo-
sexuality, the year after Reagan first mentioned AIDS in an official
speech—six years at least into the epidemic, and a time, in general, when
drug companies profiteered at the expense of PWAs (People with AIDS)
and health insurance companies abandoned those at risk. In 1987, Bill
Olander, curator at the New Museum, commissioned ACT UP members to
do an installation in the museum's front window space, *Let the Record Show*
... (fig. 7.3), and the public impact of that then-daring act was part of the

spur for the formation of a design/art group for AIDS awareness in January 1988 and the protest graphics of ten artists including designers Marlene McCarty and Donald Moffett, filmmaker Tom Kalin, and videomaker John Lindell (figs. 7.4, 7.5).

For the posters and pamphlets of the Guerrilla Girls and Gran Fury and their younger cousin WAC (Women's Action Coalition), which came on the scene a few years later, the style was to cement a hard-hitting, single-image graphic (a female nude wearing a gorilla mask, two men kissing, or an unblinking eye, for example) with a didactic, advertising-like caption ("Do women have to be naked to get into the Met?," "Kissing doesn't kill: Greed and indifference do" (fig. 7.6), and "WAC is watching," respectively). Yet for all their design simplicity, these graphics were also inflected by traits commonly assigned to postmodernism: a sense of humor and play, use of irony, and blatant appropriation of other artistic styles. In particular, the work of Barbara Kruger was often quoted (for example, by Gran Fury, as noted by Douglas Crimp and Adam Rolston in their 1990 book *AIDS Demographics*), although the collectives tended to detour around Kruger's sophisticated use of ambiguity in works such as *You construct intricate rituals which allow you to touch the skin of other men* to tap the straightforward style of her poster and media work such as her pro-choice poster *Your body is a battleground*. But the Left art world in the eighties searched for historical models as well, such as the radical twenties and thirties anti-Nazi graphics of John Heartfield.

However, in industrialized countries, ownership of the mass media—publishing houses for newspapers, books, and magazines, production companies for TV and film—were considerably more monopolized and centralized in the 1980s than in the 1920s. For artists, illustrators, caricaturists, designers, cartoonists, and other visual editorialists to have the kind of voice Heartfield had in the late 1920s and early 1930s with his covers, appearing at a rate of approximately one per month for *AIZ* (*Arbeiter Illustrierte Zeitung—Workers' Illustrated Newspaper*), one of Germany's most popular newsweeklies, was almost unheard of, due to the limited public access monopolized print media provide. Perhaps Heartfield's closest equivalents today in the United States would be Matt Groening, creator of

Group Material, *Contribution to the 1985 Whitney Biennial,*
The Whitney Museum of American Art.
**(7.7)**

the nationally broadcast, prime-time animated show *The Simpsons,* and Gary Trudeau, author of the comic strip *Doonesbury.* Extending beyond the art world, in the early 1990s, Barbara Kruger began to enter the mass-market print media world in full force. She created visual op-ed pieces for the *New York Times,* covers for *Newsweek* and *Esquire* magazines, and a fashion project for *Harper's Bazaar.* It is particularly rare and history-making for a female artist to have attained this kind of opinion-forming, mass-distribution power.

But in the mid-1980s, access to the mass media for artists seemed harder to achieve, and in retrospect I think this difficulty informed some of the Left art world's nostalgia for and interest in the Weimar artists who did enjoy a media soapbox. In addition there was a generational parallel:

the generation who came of age in the 1920s in countries like the United States and Germany celebrated a new saturation of media in everyday culture—an explosion of radio, film, and photojournalism. Analogously, the generation born soon after World War II in Western industrialized countries was the first to grow up with television. For those baby boomers who eventually joined the population of the New York art world, the daily pleasures and sophistication of TV's high-quality production and its format, plot, and advertising appropriations paved the way for an enthusiastic reading of the 1920s and 1930s writings of German cultural critics Walter Benjamin, Bertolt Brecht, Siegfried Kracauer, and Ernst Bloch. They devoured these critics who dove into popular culture, enjoyed it, and simultaneously retrieved elements of it for its own critique, much more so than sour Adorno or straight-laced Lukács. The critique from within— brought up to date with the institution-based theories of Althusser and media-focused writings like Judith Williamson's of British cultural studies—spoke to eighties artists collectives in New York City. After all, these groups were large, low-budget, cottage-industry coalitions, so the discussions of the interface of individual analyses with mass culture, in particular mass media and other cultural institutions, appealed. For these art and propaganda groups, mass media was, and is, seen as *the* powerful teaching institution where small budgets could be most economically magnified in power—or at least dreams of this were fostered. The media and its accompanying design techniques had a particular draw for single-issue groups that attempted a tight focus in order to accomplish anything politically at all during the social-service-cutting Reagan years.

How was Group Material faring, though, in the 1980s, with its more scattershot approach, curating shows, expanding artistic access to disempowered people, postering subways, and so forth? This question raises the issue of how effectively, in different ways, different models of collectivism function in an unabashedly capitalist society. I would argue that, while the small-group, community focus of Group Material's early exhibitions served its members and immediate audiences, Group Material was most broadly effective, as are other U.S. collectives, when it intersected with cultural institutions already successfully embedded in the capitalist mar-

Collectivism in the Decade of Greed

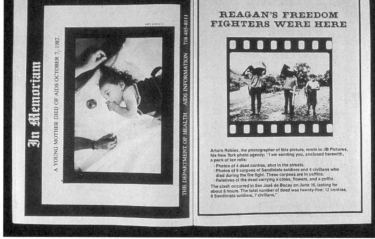

Group Material, *Inserts, The Sunday New York Times* (May 22 1988), detail Nancy Linn/Hans Haacke.
(**7.8a,b**)

ketplace—which is all a long way of saying that to have a voice in capitalism, the institutions already existing and speaking loudly must be used. These are not necessarily—or usually—collectivist tools, but can be bent for that purpose. And in fact the real stories of negotiation and compromise may be not so much about discussions within the various political collectives where members, as argumentative as they might be, tended to be like-minded, but rather in the labyrinthian contracts made on a group basis with larger, powerful organizations.

Consider Group Material's collaborations with two powerful New York art institutions, the Whitney Museum of American Art and the Dia Art Foundation, and the group's occasional infiltration of the mass media. In the 1985 Whitney Biennial where, like all Whitney Biennials, selection of the artists was highly disputed and status-conscious, Group Material snuck an additional forty-five artists representing a truly democratic mix of styles into their installation to create a crowded, quite popular Biennial-within-a-Biennial (fig. 7.7). For the Dia Art Foundation in 1988–89, Group Material organized a series of public "town meetings" (discussion forums) and exhibitions around democratic themes, particularly education, participation, and politics. These Whitney and Dia events served an art world public but spilled into the media as well with fairly comprehensive coverage. Group Material directly contributed to the media when, on May 22, 1988, it produced an insert in *The Sunday New York Times*, a twelve-page, paid-for supplement including works by ten invited artists known as media strategists such as Jenny Holzer, Carrie Mae Weems, and Hans Haacke (figs. 7.8a,b). Funded by the Public Art Fund, the New York State Council for the Arts, and Art Matters, *Inserts* was handled by the *Times* advertising department, and Group Material had to negotiate with the Advertising Acceptability Editor to get the content approved. The cost for 115,000 inserts (about one-tenth of the *Sunday Times* circulation) was approximately $17,000. In an unprecedented marshaling of art magazines, Group Material, with Visual AIDS (a political group promoting AIDS awareness), published an AIDS timeline in 1990 in *Afterimage, Art & Auction, Art in America, Arts, October, Parkett*, and five other venues combining historical facts about the epidemic, artworks, reports on government actions and inactions, and safe sex information. Individual editors were approached, and the magazines each donated the space involved.

The focus on the media, though, was more than an 1980s trend and continued with artists' organizations into the nineties, through George Bush's term (1988–92) and the more liberal Clinton era. A nineties example is the short-lived Barbie Liberation Organization (B.L.O.) which worked with a kind of warped consumerism and media-savviness. It was a group that deftly exploited already flourishing shopping-mall culture.

The Barbie Liberation Organization, an East Village–based performance art group, whose members were anonymous, splashed into the media for a brief time around Christmas 1993. They had bought some three hundred Barbie and G.I. Joe dolls and surgically altered them by trading the masculine and feminine voice boxes. The retreaded Barbies said things like "Eat lead, Cobra!" and "Attack!" and the tampered G.I. Joes trilled "Let's go shopping!" and "Let's plan our dream wedding!" Then the B.L.O. placed the sabotaged dolls back on store shelves in a couple of different areas of the United States where they were bought by unsuspecting customers who received as well a pamphlet in every box decrying sexism and violence in the toy industry and asking people to call their local media. Media coverage across the country was astounding; the B.L.O. managed both to entertain and to plug into parents' anxiety about their children's consumer culture. As one answer to the question about how politically oriented collectives can function in a rambunctiously capitalist society, the B.L.O. managed to participate temporarily in institutions of retail consumerism and media entertainment, thereby getting out a message of reform.

Members of the B.L.O. needed to remain anonymous because they were engaged in illegal, if not criminal, activities—redesigning a product and putting it back on the shelves. The Guerrilla Girls also have feared retribution—but by peers and authorities in the arts who might seek to damage individual careers, not by the government—and their anonymity is a sadder index of how little power women artists actually do have in the art world. A Guerrilla Girl told Mira Schor: "Publishing our names would destroy our anonymity, and therefore both our effectivity and our careers would be gone, dead."[1] Ironically, the Guerrilla Girls use naming and shaming as a technique to pressure galleries and other organizations into showing and selling art by women and racial minorities, as in their 1985 poster *These galleries show no more than 10% women artists or none at all* fingering Leo Castelli, Marlborough, and others (fig. 7.9). Occasionally, Group Material's members will sign their names to statements, but much of their work and the products of other groups like Gran Fury and WAC are authored by the coalition's name and not those of individual artists.

As much as I respect each of these collectives, examining them, as well as having attended WAC meetings, has raised a general question for me: is anonymity sometimes counterproductive? Perhaps an eschewing of individualism can be inhibiting. When creative coalitions are composed of many people who already lack power and name recognition, many of whom have to work day jobs and do their own work at night in order to pay New York City's high rents, and are nonprofit to boot, they can foster a certain kind of bitterness, a feeling that there's a lot of work but little reward. On the one hand, in idealistic, purist structures where all decisions are made collectively, there is no hierarchy, and the lack of pandering to individual egos can seem a welcome rebellion, a break from our voraciously commodified society where authors/artists function as one more commodity. On the other hand, this relief can be temporary and is often replaced by exhaustion and infighting. Many people operate better with

**Collectivism in the Decade of Greed**

Guerilla Girls, *These galleries show no more than 10% women artists or none at all,* poster, 1985. This was one of "the posters that started it all. We plastered them on the walls of Soho in the middle of the night."

**(7.9)**

*Names Project AIDS Memorial Quilt,* Washington, D.C.,
Oct. 10–11, 1992, photograph by Jonathan Weinberg.
**(7.10)**

the fuel of ego boosts. It is difficult, in a society where people are raised
to expect consumerist rewards for working, to receive so little in terms of
recognition or money, and at times the satisfaction of long-term teaching
through the media can seem too distant. There can be a kind of puritanism
to the anonymity that seems forced and joyless, repressing strong authorial emotions that go into the forming of political art collectives. People
often enjoy identifying with their own anger, take pleasure in speaking
out, and find satisfaction in influencing the media and/or legislation. My
position, and personal experience, is that purist models of collectivism are
not as effective in the United States as those that work with existing capitalist institutions, and that often include using some form of authorship.
This pragmatic approach involves individual satisfaction as well as group
effort: in general my bias is against anonymity.

In conclusion, let one strong example of the melding of deep emotion, name honoring, individual closure, and the continuity of coalition
political beliefs—the AIDS quilt—stand as a model for a profoundly

effective kind of art and politics collectivism. Begun in 1987 by San Francisco–based gay activist Cleve Jones, the AIDS quilt (officially titled the Names Project AIDS Memorial Quilt) is made up of three-by-six-foot panels, each commemorating the death of one person and signed by the creator of the panel (fig. 7.10). It is more than a mourning shroud. Funded by the Names Project Foundation, the quilt (or parts of it) tours the country making a powerful if implicit statement—interpreted by lobbyists and casual observers as well—about the need for government spending on medical research, reform of health insurance policies, and tightening of drug company regulation. Through the efforts of the quiltmakers, ACT UP, and other AIDS activist groups (along with the experience and voices of the many Americans who live without health insurance), it has now become common wisdom that health care in the United States is unfairly distributed. These collectives, artistic and otherwise, without a doubt contributed to the attempt of the Clinton administration during its first two years to make health reform a priority and to the continuing public awareness of health care and insurance problems. All the while, the AIDS quilt honors the individual lives that have been lost and appreciates the creativity, emotions, and collective action of those who remain alive.

**Note**

1. Mira Schor, "Girls Will Be Girls,"*Artforum* (Sept. 1990): 124–129.

# Portfolio: Women and Design

In the first decades of the twentieth century when photography became well established as a commercial field, women streamed into the new profession. The reasons are easy to see—there was only a scant old-boy network to infiltrate; to some degree work could be pursued independently outside of hierarchies; the new technology and the means to reach large audiences were compelling. At the same time, graphic design began to grow as a profession, one closely intertwined with the promotion of corporate identity, and this growth then accelerated after World War II. Although tied closely to predominantly male-run corporations and populated mainly by men, the graphic design field also has proved appealing for women: its newness made it relatively free of male guilds and open to a cottage-industry approach. Like photographers, designers have been involved with new technologies and broad audiences. As women's overall participation in the U.S. job market soared in the last two decades of the twentieth century, women have increasingly entered the graphic design field. In fact, the American Institute of Graphic Design has estimated that as of the 1990s, women peopled the field in higher numbers than men.[1]

Women in graphic design, however, still do not earn as much as men in the field, and, while the gap seems to be closing, differences in money and power at top-earning, corporate-service levels of the profession are significant. The self-employment picture differs by gender as well, with women earning less than men. More women than

men are free-lance graphic designers. More men are owners/designers in firms that hire others. Differences in earnings, though, do not comprise the whole picture of how gender inflects the contemporary design world.

Design historian and designer Martha Scotford has found through her survey work that women designers are more likely than men to pursue design careers that allow them to use design for personal, political, or social agendas.[2] However, although many women, and some men, may express these goals, pressures of time and money make most design practices client-service dominated. There is, in fact, only a small subset of designers who are able to make "personal, political, or social agendas" a high priority. Although male designers who create for personal or political reasons also stand out—Art Chantry in Seattle and St. Louis with his political posters and J. Abbott Miller in New York with his journal *Twice* are just two examples—most of the leaders in this politically and self-expressive subset of the field are women, such as Sylvia Harris, Ellen McMahon, and Marlene McCarty.

I grew particularly interested in the self-generated work the women in this subset were doing—and in how they managed in a traditionally client-oriented field to pay their bills while keeping self-generated design as a high priority. I wondered how "multitasking" played into the mix. "Multitasking" has become a common word in our culture since the rise of the computer, but in the design world it carries the specific meaning of producing many kinds of design using many kinds of technology for many kinds of venues. And what about the nuts and bolts of billing? If women are still being paid less in design, wouldn't that give them less money with which to pursue independent projects?

I posed my questions to female designers known for their self-generated work and/or authorial voices. Specifically, I asked them: (1) In order to carve out time to create self-generated work, how do you balance the various pieces of your practice—work for clients and work for yourself? What kind of work do you love to initiate?; (2) Do you see this kind of multitasking practice spreading throughout the field? Gaining popularity with women designers in particular? Any thoughts on this?; and (3) At this point in time, do you see the fact that you're a woman influencing any of the labor practices you're involved in? For instance, do you experience a difference in pay from male designers? What I heard in response altered my assumptions about process but confirmed my impressions about priorities. I had assumed a more clear trade-off between work done for love and work for money, and what I found were practices where the two types of work were often—though not always—blended.

The following selection of designers and their work reflects a number of different production models—that is, different processes for designers to articulate authorship, while also earning a living. (The issue of authorship has a particular meaning in the design field. Since virtually all work is for a client, even if sometimes an unconventional one like a zine, the idea of a single author who creates work that is completely self-initiated and produced, the concept of the lone creator so popular in the art world, rarely applies. Instead "authorial voice" in design is a more subjective concept and signifies a designer's impact on her work in such a way that the designer's style and content are evident. This sounds mild, but achieving this kind of authorial stamp, particularly a stamp on content, is exactly the opposite of the traditional role of the designer, which is only to enhance the client's message.)

Many of the designers represented in the following portfolio have chosen to teach, either part-time or full-time, in order to become less client-dependent; Lorraine Wild, Lucille Tenazas, and Ellen Lupton are examples. Some of these women such as Tenazas maintain an active client-oriented practice as well but are able to be quite selective about clients. Designers like Denise Gonzales Crisp, at the Art Center in Pasadena, and Paula Scher, at Pentagram, are able to work with clients in creative collaborations that allow the designers great flexibility. Other designers—Marlene McCarty, Ann Tyler, and Ellen McMahon—use the artist model of production, showing in and selling through galleries as well as, in some cases, teaching and/or doing corporate design. Still others, such as Fo Wilson with furniture design, are diversifying the kinds of design they do. New media provide yet another marketplace for producers such as Peggy Weil.

Even though all the designers interviewed agreed they have multi-tasking practices, my questions about multitasking, however, did not primarily elicit responses about designing for different types of clients. Instead, concerns expressed in this area were often about balancing work and family and about combining work that was completely self-generated with work that was not. The ideal often expressed by those with children was to be self-employed and in control so as to most efficiently perform triage. In the late 1990s, both Lucille Tenazas and Jessica Helfand, for instance, combined work and family spaces so they'd be contiguous.

The women represented in this portfolio were not for the most part experiencing gender discrimination in pay—nor was this a primary concern. They reported that money concerns had weight—money to pay the bills and to buy time for self-generated projects—but they did not perceive their earnings to be less than that of their male counterparts. However, my guess is that this topic resonated less than the others because these women are quite successful in their field(s) and so are able to bill at rates comparable to those of their male peers. Looking at the field earning statistics as a whole, though, I found that this is not the case for all women designers.

Even for the group of women represented here, money issues were complex, when viewed through a gender lens. A number reported that maximizing earnings was not a top priority. They felt they were more interested in self-fulfillment and making a political difference than were their male colleagues who were more focused on making money—even though in most cases the women interviewed here were either the primary breadwinners for themselves and/or their families or integral breadwinners for their families. This raises questions about other issues including but beyond the design field about how men and women in the United States are socialized differently with regard to money, a difference that persists despite changes in women's participation in the workforce. (As of 1995, the Whirlpool Foundation reported that "a majority of employed women—55 percent—provide all (18 percent), more than half (11 percent), or about half (26 percent) of their households' incomes."[3] The designer Paula Scher also points out that female designers have not yet made significant inroads in lucrative Fortune 500 design work. So sociological questions of women, money, and self-generated design work are chicken and egg: is it because women are still denied top dollar in the field that they are "free" to set other priorities, or is it because they have other priorities that certain women are doing more interesting but less plush work than designing corporate logos?

The following portfolio serves as an introduction to the group of U.S.-based women who are leaders in achieving authorial voice in design and to the different models of production they've evolved to make possible self-generated or largely self-generated work. In it, I've excerpted quotes from the designers' individual responses—some chose to respond at length, some briefly. I chose these passages to emphasize individual solutions to the general issues raised. It is important, I feel, to hear directly from the designers, because even though their practices represent categorical models of production, often an overlapping of several, their approaches are also individual—fascinating and complex negotiations of asserting authorial voice while also earning a living at this point in design history. In their responses, the designers variously articulate the cultural politics and individual excitement of addressing these challenges.

## Portfolio

**Caryn Aono** (fig. 8.1)

Works in Valencia, Calif.; art director, California Institute of the Arts—responsible for design of Institute identity, capital campaign, performance publicity, annual report, and publications; free-lance clients include Wieden & Kennedy and the Japanese American National Museum; also teaches graphic design at CalArts.

"I work in-house for an art college as their art director. The design work I do for Institute clients usually reflects the progressive nature of those departments. I'm fortunate to do my work in an experimental environment where new forms, technologies, and vocabularies are encouraged and embraced. Thus in my work I am able to combine client-based work with my personal areas of study."

Caryn Aono, *CalArts Spring Music Festival*, poster, 1995.
(**8.1**)

**Sheila Levrant de Bretteville** (fig. 8.2)

Works in New Haven and Hamden, Conn.; professor and director of studies in graphic design, School of Art, Yale University; her studio is The Sheila Studio, Hamden, Conn.

"I do permanent installations on subjects I choose and in public spaces. This work is self-generated in the sense that I make a proposal regarding what I would want to make, what materials I want to use, the content of the images, and the texts. If the public art commission—usually made up of people from the neighborhood—and the cultural affairs commission pick me, I get to do just what I believe should be done there.

"Because my practice is now entirely self-generated work in terms of content, materials, and forms, I have only to find the time in relation to my teaching schedule at Yale. What I love most about this work is that I can go to a site and imagine what could be there and as long as it fits the budget allotted I can make what I imagine happen. I have never had to compromise, but I have had to persevere to get it done the way I wanted mostly by putting in an inordinate number of hours at the site. This is not an economically viable way to do this work, so I've used teaching to support this work."

Sheila Levrant de Bretteville, *Julia Di Lullo Star, Path of Stars,* installation, New Haven, 1994.
**(8.2)**

BUST (fig. 8.3)

Zine/magazine published in New York, N.Y.; art director Laurie Henzel, editors Marcelle Karp and Debbie Stoller.

Laurie Henzel works in New York and is a freelance designer of CD and record covers. She's been art director/founding member of BUST since 1993.

"In BUST, I work with my editors to come up with the theme and the image, so I feel lucky because this is both commercial and personal work for me. I love doing BUST because so far there hasn't been any pressure to have the work look a certain way—only my own ideas or restrictions about how I feel the work should look."

From Marcelle Karp and Debbie Stoller's introduction to their *The BUST Guide to the New Girl Order:*[4]

"'A Day in the Life' was the first issue of BUST. It was only 29 (count 'em!) pages long, and we made five hundred copies, Xeroxing and stapling till our wrists ached. Shortly after we had gotten it out there into the world, we started getting fan mail from readers, submissions for our next issue and more orders (we ended up making another five hundred copies). It was then that we began to realize that we were onto something big. Inspired by the first issue's success, we pooled our money together so that we could actually print the next issue all professional-like, and asked a groovy designer, Laurie Henzel, who we knew from our Big Media Conglomerate days, to join us as a third partner in crime. With an art director to guide us, BUST finally began to develop into a magazine whose look was as brazen as its voice. . . .

"Five years down the line, BUST has developed from an AA cup to a C cup, and we continue to grow. We've increased our distribution . . . to 32,000 copies, a small step for magazines, but a giant leap for zinekind. We take whatever money we make—from subscribers, sales, advertising—and invest it into the next issue, growing BUST step-by-step from a handmade rag into a full-on glossy mag with color. Our lives have changed dramatically, but still not enough to give up our day jobs. BUST continues, to this day, to be a labor of love. . . .

**Portfolio**

"In BUST, we've captured the voice of a brave new girl: one that is raw and real, straightforward and sarcastic, smart and silly, and liberally sprinkled with references to our own Girl Culture—that shared set of female expectations that includes Barbies and blowjobs, sexism and shoplifting, *Vogue* and vaginas."

*BUST* zine, cover of "My Life as a Girl" Issue 5 (Winter/Spring 1995). Art director: Areola (Laurie Henzel); editors: Marcelle Karp and Debbie Stoller.
(**8.3**)

**Denise Gonzales Crisp** (fig. 8.4)

Works in Pasadena, Calif.; design director, Art Center College of Design, and teaches typography and other graphic design courses part-time there; earlier work in corporate design for Cummings Design Partnership and Pritikin Programs, both in Santa Monica.

"As the senior designer for Art Center College of Design, I'm fortunate in that I've been asked to incorporate my sensibilities with the promotional needs of the school and with its changing identity. While I wouldn't describe designing an identity system for an educational institution as personal work, I willfully infuse myself in the work, enough I guess to make personal projects less imperative. I do, however, participate in projects that allow more unfettered exploration. For instance, right now I'm redesigning the international art magazine *art/text* for very little pay. The publisher understands that the design decisions are there to reveal my hand as the designer as much as to establish a new identity for the 19-year-strong publication.

"I created the *Graphesis* prototype in 1996 during my last semester as an MFA candidate at CalArts. It's a design magazine and the intent is to explore the relationship between form and idea in hopes of expanding what designers can do, and how designers can think about what they do. Visual form is integrated with written form; the visual lends meaning to words through form. I wanted to promote different ways of thinking and writing about graphic design. I continue to be dedicated to pragmatic play, to the fusion of writing and design, in order to get at graphic design issues differently."

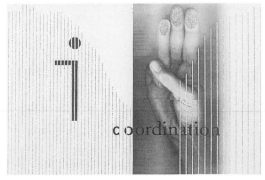

**Portfolio**

Denise Gonzales Crisp, *Graphesis,* a prototype magazine, 1996.
**(8.4)**

**Barbara Glauber** (fig. 8.5)

Works in New York, N.Y.: principal, Heavy Meta; teaches design part-time at Yale.

"I curated and designed the exhibition *Lift and Separate: Graphic Design and the Quote Unquote Vernacular* and edited the monograph. Most of the essayists designed their own pages, and I designed the rest of the book. The 66-page monograph and exhibition explore the complex relationship between the so-called vernacular and the contemporary graphic designer. The ten essays explore the hierarchy, appropriation, and recontextualization of various visual dialects, including skateboard subculture, the graphic landscape of roadside American signage, and the use of nostalgic imagery. Most of the contributors are practicing graphic designers whose visual voices are expressed through the design of their articles.

"But I don't have much time to do self-generated work. I teach one day a week in the graduate graphic design program at Yale and find that that's where any of that spare nonprofit time and energy goes. While it provides me with contact with talented people who are asking a lot of interesting questions about making design—unlike most of my clients—

Barbara Glauber, curator and catalog designer, *Lift and Separate: Graphic Design and the Quote Unquote Vernacular*, The Herb Lubalin Study Center of Design and Typography, Cooper Union, New York, 1993.
**(8.5)**

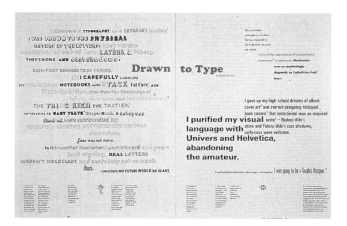

it can also be a bit frustrating when the limitations of my commercial work don't allow for the same type of conceptual explorations I encourage my students to pursue. However, designing engaging and critical assignments and seeing how students address them can be extremely rewarding.

"In my studio, I try to pull out a few projects a year from my enormous workload in which the combination of content, client, and medium could provide a springboard for my own visual and conceptual explorations and then invest a significant, money-losing amount of time designing them. Sometimes this works.

"My multitasking addiction manifests itself in a kind of diversity of media, clients, audiences, and scale in the projects I undertake professionally. I'd hate to make any generalizations about the multitasking nature of the lives of women, but as I sit here nine months pregnant and anxious about everything from epidurals to page layouts to coffee tables, it's certainly true for me personally. Perhaps multitasking is just the cybernineties euphemism for Superwoman."

**Sylvia Harris** (fig. 8.6)
Works in New York, N.Y.; planning consultant specializing in large public information design projects; critic in the graduate graphic design program at Yale; former principal of 212 Associates, New York City; contributed to the design of Census 2000 from 1992–97.

Sylvia Harris's involvement in Census 2000 is a story both impressive and frustrating. In 1992, Harris participated in a design round table organized by the Clinton administration where she articulated her goal to improve census participation through creating better designed forms. In a formidable display of perseverance, she then began to insert herself in the census design process. First she worked with her Yale students and the New Haven Census Bureau to create new prototypes. Harris then approached the federal office where she was appointed first as an advisor and then, working with her former partners at 212 Associates, was hired by Director Martha Riche to redesign the census. Harris and 212 worked with mail specialist Don

Dillman (the 2000 census is the largest direct mail campaign in U.S. history) and focus groups to reach some surprising conclusions, for instance, that an "official-looking" design achieved a better response rate than a cheery-looking one, which appeared too much like consumer mailings. Harris also developed a brand identity for Census 2000—consistent elements like a logo. However, after Director Riche left amid Congressional disagreements about sampling procedures, Harris's influence waned. At the end of 1997, Harris and 212 had their contract canceled. Nevertheless elements of their design such as the logo were employed in Census 2000.[5]

"Well-paying work always offsets the projects done for love. When I had a studio, I would take on one exhibit project at a time. I enjoy African American history and have always wanted to contribute to the making of this history. By always having one exhibit project in the gate, I could do it, but not be overwhelmed.

"I have not experienced much discrimination as a woman in the field. I think I have come along at a good time and have not worked as an employee. As a business owner, people hire you based on track record. Once again, the main thing I see in this profession as well as others is the

Sylvia Harris, creative director, *Census 2000 forms,* as of December 1997.
(**8.6**)

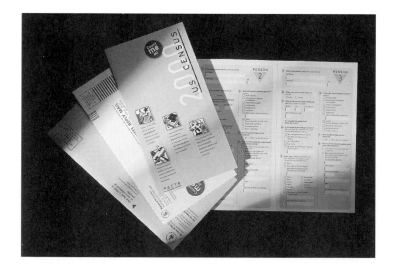

men have the liberty to be very single-minded about their careers. It seems like women are multitasking their practices and kids. Many women I know my age have given up big demanding practices to work at home in a more flexible setting. Is it more to be close to kids or are they disillusioned with the design biz in general and have more permission to walk away? Not sure. For me it was a bit of both."

**Jessica Helfand** (fig. 8.7a,b)
Works in Falls Village, Conn.; partner since 1997 in Jessica Helfand/William Drenttel, Inc., for four years previous to that had her own studio, Jessica Helfand Studio, Ltd., specializing in new media design; columnist for *Eye* magazine, teaches design part-time at Yale.

"What I'm finding is that self-generated work is increasingly not graphic design work. By way of example, I have written the first 100 pages of a novel—set in the design world—as a way to break out of the conventions of criticism that have framed my writing for nearly a decade. It's like flexing a different muscle: wonderfully liberating and a little scary.

"Carving out time seems to be a challenge for most people, and in my case, it is not only about my work and the practice, but also my work with respect to my family. We moved out of New York a year ago and are in the process of renovating our studio, attached to our house, built into the mountain ledge on ten acres at the foot of the Berkshires. The studio was built in the 1930s for American muralist Ezra Winter: it's 32 feet high with 25-foot-high windows facing north. This is a dramatic change from working in NYC, from living in NYC, and has everything to do with our wanting to redefine the boundaries between home and studio. So our children breathe fresh air, and we see them periodically through the day—rather than before and after the preordained 'working' hours of 9 a.m. and 6 p.m. Ironically we now have clients in far-flung places like San Francisco and London, so we are juggling quite a bit of travel into this scenario. Carving out time for anything seems a difficult thing to do for us lately.

**Portfolio**

"That said, I am interested in initiating projects in which design is positioned less as a service and more as a conceptual toolkit, design variables being the common currency that facilitate or simplify a discussion, that streamline or clarify a set of problems. For example, Bill [Drenttel] and I have filed a patent on a design system for screen-based media that is predicated on the idea of the Tatami—the double square—as a recombinant geometric grid system. In an environment as dynamic (and chaotic) as electronic media, the value of a set of harmoniously proportioned templates has a kind of renewed value, presenting itself as a sort of underlying armature, a basis for a kind of design logic. We've just licensed this system to Rupert Murdoch on behalf of *The* [New York] *Times* and *The Sunday Times* of London: we are designing a set of Web sites for these newspapers and consulting on a series of more 'e-commerce'-based

Jessica Helfand and William Drentell, *TatamiNet*™, grid studies and grid application, 1999. Grid studies: Compositional permutations based on TatamiNet™ family of grids. TatamiNet™ is a system for computer screen composition based on the recombinant modular geometrics of the Japanese Tatami mat. Grid application: TatamiNet™ used as the underlying armature for a Web site for networked teaching. Here, a student is asked to select a template for one of a series of reports.
(**8.7a,b**)

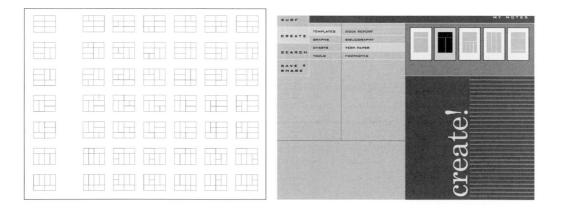

businesses for Murdoch's NewsCorp. So, folding in the Tatami idea (it's actually called TatamiNet) is, I think, a good example of what you describe as 'work created in cooperation with a client but whose concept is largely self-generated.'"

**Bethany Johns** (fig. 8.8a,b)

Works in New York, N.Y.; principal of Bethany Johns Design; critic/lecturer, Yale graduate graphic design program; recent book design projects include catalogs for San Francisco Museum of Modern Art, Carnegie Museum of Art, and Site Santa Fe.

"I guess the graphic work created for WAC (Women's Action Coalition)— the quick cheap production of graphics to use in our direct actions—represents the closest thing to 'self-generated work' despite its close alignment with all the things I experience in my design practice—the presentation of a design idea to a group, the incorporation of corrections or adjustments, the final form of it concocted under enormous time and money constraints. The difference I suppose is in the work's origins coming from my own 'voice' instead of the transmission of another's.

"Since all my professional work is for not-for-profits such as art museums, foundations, and individual arts/education groups, there often seems to be very little difference in how content sorts out into work for clients and work for myself, if I consider the essence of the work for WAC 'work for myself.' It's all about content. When I think of what constitutes 'my own work' it rests largely on this choice of content—and on joining in force with others to voice a message clearly. So the distinctions blur somewhat. I feel less desire and need to create 'art objects' or individual design projects the more I get to work alongside people who through their own art or writing or music align themselves with the kind of content I'm preoccupied with. And I do end up with a shelf of handsome things I actually enjoy reading and going back to.

"Surely there's more money to be made out there. I think (like many women designers) I keep my business small in order to build and keep direct relationships, but the fallout of this is that I end up doing everything from the design to the billing. Certainly there are better ways to manage a studio and there are consultants out there to help do it. The times I have approached the topic, the question rises: have you considered taking on more commercial work? The implication is that one can do less work for more money, and faster, which somehow never ends up being the case, once you've tried on a brochure project for the likes of American Express or a series of ads for Bendel. You find yourself on a cell phone at the printer at midnight debating the proper PMS color for the corporate logo, or you're skipping a dinner date to release a disk for film output after twenty rounds of changes in one sentence describing a shade of lipstick."

Bethany Johns and Marlene McCarty, *WAC is Watching*, WAC logo, and Bethany Johns and the WAC Lesbian Caucus, *KD Lang*, poster image, both 1992. (8.8a,b)

**Barbara Kruger (**fig. 8.9a–e)

Works in Los Angeles, Calif., and New York, N.Y.; 1999 retrospective at the Museum of Contemporary Art, Los Angeles. Kruger created this image and word series for *Harper's Bazaar* in 1994. After art school (she went to Parsons School of Design where she studied with magazine art director Marvin Israel), Kruger worked for eleven years as an assistant art director and then photoeditor at fashion magazines. Kruger quit magazines in the late seventies to teach and concentrate on her art. She's best known for her photomontage art captioned with sharp-tongued slogans ("It's a small world but not if you have to clean it"), and she shows at New York's Mary Boone Gallery. But she also persists in targeting audiences beyond the art world: In recent years, for example, she's created visual op-ed pieces for *The New York Times*, political posters for the pro-choice movement, merchandise and advertising (billboards, graphics, MTV spots) funded by the Liz Claiborne Company to get needed information to women suffering from domestic violence, and a permanent installation on history and nationalism for a new train station in Strasbourg, France.

"I never really considered myself a designer. I just didn't have what it takes. I think good designers have the incredible ability, through various fluencies, to create someone else's image of perfection, to solve problems, be

constantly 'creative,' promote concerns and move the 'merch.' I think I've tried to appropriate the means and instrumentality of design practices on a formal level, but to alter the concerns of the enterprise, to some degree."

Pages 125-126:
Barbara Kruger, *Who do you think you are?; What do you want?; How much money do you make?; What are you looking at?; Who do you love?; Harper's Bazaar* (Feb. 1994): 149–153. Courtesy of *Harper's Bazaar.*
(**8.9 a–e**)

**Ellen Lupton** (fig. 8.10)

Works in Baltimore, Md., and New York, N.Y.; adjunct curator of contemporary design, Cooper-Hewitt, National Design Museum, New York City; chair, graphic design, Maryland Institute, College of Art, Baltimore.

"I initiate exhibitions and books. All my work is self-initiated, but within the context of the mother ship, Cooper Hewitt, National Design Museum.

"The big multitasking issue for me is kids/work. Many women choose to work at home and/or work part-time in order to get a better balance. There is a loss of pay associated with this, but an enormous gain in efficiency. I work at home because I avoid office politics, stupid meetings, getting into silly 'personal'/'professional' tiffs with people that waste time and energy. The result: I get more done, waste less time, see my kids more, and get paid less."

Ellen Lupton, curator, laundry line installation in *Mechanical Brides* exhibition. Designers: Ellen Lupton, Laurene Leon, and Constantin Boym. Cooper-Hewitt, National Design Museum, 1993. **(8.10)**

**Marlene McCarty**  (fig. 8.11)

Works in New York, N.Y.; member of Gran Fury and co-founder of Bureau; exhibitions include one-woman exhibition in 1993 at Metro Pictures, N.Y., and the 1999 show *Billboard* at MASS MoCA, N. Adams, Mass.; Bureau's work includes film title design for films by Todd Haynes and Cindy Sherman.

"'Balance' usually means I do the work I love at night. I often do client work during the day because that's when they have to be in contact with you. BUT things are basically always in flux. I do try to work on the work I WANT to work on at least two full days a week."

Marlene McCarty, *Hearth,* detail of 15,000 matchbooks, 1992.
**(8.11)**

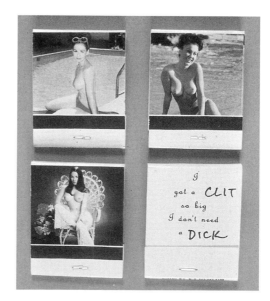

Katherine McCoy (fig. 8.12)

Works in Chicago, Ill.; senior lecturer, Illinois Institute of Technology's Institute of Design, Chicago; from 1971–95 co-chair of Cranbrook Academy of Art's Department of Design.

"I really do not do much self-generated work, probably because I continue to love the rigor of solving a client's problem and challenging the parameters and limitations of a project. I enjoy cultivating a productive relationship with a truly enlightened client, and find my clients can also be a source of new design ideas. However, I do chose my projects very carefully. Because I am selective and take projects only on referral, this means I must support my practice with other activities, such as teaching. But this is

Katherine McCoy, *Choice*, a page from the *Electronic Exquisite Corpse*, published by Gilbert Paper, 1993. Designer: Katherine McCoy; project direction: Rick Valicenti, Thirst, Chicago: "The goal of reproductive choice and personal autonomy is poised over the alternatives of salvation (water) and torment (fire). This was the final step in a collaborative project between nine designers in which each sent a page design on computer disk to the next designer in a three-step sequence. The two previous steps sent to me by two male designers, Neville Brody of England and Malcolm Enright of Australia, contained the fire and young woman images in different contexts."
(**8.12**)

fine, since teaching is also a continual source of new ideas about design that enrich my personal practice.

"Anyone who has cared for a young child and attempted to continue working, whether it be domestic or professional, knows how essential multitasking is. I am thinking that women, in their traditional role as homemaker and nurturer, always worked in this mode. Recent studies of gender differences in brain 'wiring' seem to indicate that women's brains are actually configured to accommodate this mode, whereas men's are more geared to total focus—a useful feature for battle or hunting. Certainly our family is evidence to this theory! Interestingly, just this week at a conference at IBM dedicated to emergent trends in pervasive computing, a presenter suggested that women's brains may be better suited to deal with our new world of multimedia, multiple channels and information overload—and that we could see a reversal from male-dominated economy to a woman-dominated economy.

"In terms of my own practice, I definitely have chosen a pluralistic menu of professional activities. I find a rich combination of selective professional practice, teaching and writing on design criticism and history is ideal for me. And in professional practice, I also prefer a mix of disciplines, including graphic design, signage, interior design, and some industrial design. I found that teaching and writing are critical to my growth as a designer, and so chose to make less income in order to pursue these as well as design practice."

Ellen McMahon (fig. 8.13)
Works in Tucson, Ariz.; associate professor, Deptartment of Art, University of Arizona, Tucson, teaches graphic design; solo exhibitions include *Redressing the Mother* (1997), A.I.R., New York, and *Maternity, Autonomy, Ambivalence and Loss* (1996), Vermont College, Montpelier.

"Over the past several years my work has explored the points of collision between my experience of mothering and my expectations, based on cultural constructions, of that role.

"For instance, on one level the project *Baby Talk* flash cards (fig. 8.13) is lightly ironic—a pack of flash cards designed to teach grown ups how to talk baby talk. At the same time, on a deeper level, the text on the box acknowledges the frustration and underlying rage that parents feel who have sublimated their own subjectivities to the tyrant infant. The text also gently invites the caretaker to try out some of those effective infant strategies with additional products such as 'Guide to Having Your Own Temper Tantrum,' 'How to Fall Asleep Anywhere,' and 'Getting Your Needs Met Instantly.' The proceeds from sales go to the Parents' Support Fund, which provides parents with information and skills to support their work as parents and assistance in building support networks for their families.

"I started doing self-generated work in 1990 when I was hired as a tenure-track assistant professor. I had two daughters (one three weeks old and one five years old) and was hired to teach full-time and also to direct the visual communications program. I had a small design and illustration practice.

Ellen McMahon, *Baby Talk* and *Pre-Verbal* flash cards and covers, 1998.
**(8.13)**

"Under these circumstances my time and energy became incredibly precious. I stopped working for clients and started determining the content of all of my work. Since I was making a living at the university, I didn't need the money I was getting from client-based work, but I needed national recognition in my field to get tenure. I didn't want to do that through design competitions so I took a chance and started a body of personal work about my experience of motherhood. At the time I didn't know if it would be considered 'design' or 'art,' or whether I would get tenured based on it. But I needed the satisfaction of making work about my own experience and the perspective that brought to my daily life. I also felt compelled to bring issues to the surface that might contribute to a new understanding of the social category of mother (which I felt oppressed, confused and overwhelmed by). Recently I've started doing some design for nonprofit organizations that support women and families now that I'm tenured and my children are getting older.

"I expect my students to create a multitasking practice that will pay the bills, satisfy them personally, and have the social and political ramifications that they want. I think the incorporation of relevant self-expression in their client-based work will make it more satisfying to them, more interesting to the client, and more effective with the audience. Traditionally women have been conditioned to be better at multitasking, but the benefits are clear enough that men (especially in the generation of my students) are quickly catching up."

Rebeca Méndez (fig. 8. 14)
Works in S. Pasadena, Calif.; principal, Rebeca Méndez Communication Design; former creative director of the Art Center College of Design's design office; still teaches communication design part-time at the Art Center; clients include Wieden and Kennedy for Microsoft and ARKRestaurants for Tsunami in Las Vegas.

"Carving time to create self-generated work needs to be merciless and unforgiving—one fast swerve away from other responsibilities and not looking back, not for one instant, not for one phone call, or the vital space is pierced and the vital juices leak out. I find executing this determined move to be of great difficulty, for my business demands so much of me.

"Sometimes, when appropriate, I use client work or teaching as a springboard to personal work. In 1999, I co-taught a class with broadcast designer Rick Morris in digital filmmaking, and we purposely made our contribution to be also a tangible product—a digital video based on the Greek myth of Orpheus. This six-minute short premiered at the RESFEST in November '99 and traveled to six major worldwide cities including New York and Tokyo. Sometimes it feels like a superhuman effort to run your studio during the day and work on personal projects during the night and weekends.

"I don't find it to be an achievement to focus only on the amount of money I may receive for a project. Mostly I find a feeling of achievement in how the creative process enables me to live at my full potential."

Rebeca Méndez and Rick Morris, directors, *Orpheus re: visited*, six-minute digital video, 1999.
**(8.14)**

**Paula Scher** (fig. 8.15)

Works in New York, N.Y.; partner, Pentagram; the only woman of the 16 partners; among her many clients is New York City's Public Theater whose image she redesigned.

"All of my work for the Public Theater has been done in collaboration with the theater's director, George C. Wolfe. While the posters have to accurately reflect the spirit of the plays, how they do so is really left to me.

"I think it is irrelevant whether work is self-initiated or not. What I think matters is for a designer to have a sense of authorship. When a self-generated project is published, a designer still must collaborate in some capacity with the publishing company, and that's not terribly different from a positive client/designer relationship.

"I have found that my work really breaks down into two categories: work that I do for lots of money and work that I do for a lot less money. The work that I do for lots of money generally involves big groups of people in complicated structures, found in corporations or large institutions. In these situations, I'm being paid not for design, but to make the various players comfortable with the idea of making a relatively subjec-

Paula Scher, *Hamlet Poster,* Public Theater/New York Shakespeare Festival, 1999.
**(8.15)**

tive, visual change. Because so many people (usually indecisive and fearful) are involved, my work tends to become watered down by committee and I have lost my authorship.

"I choose to do work for less money, that is, pro-bono, for not-for-profit organizations or self-generated projects, and so forth, to maintain control and authorship of my work. Very often these projects become as politically complicated as the high-paying ones, and I lose the authorship anyway.

"I like to initiate anything that allows my individual voice to come through, either aesthetically or in content. I call this the passion for making things or making things up, and I'm equally happy doing it for a client as for myself. I try to do it as much as possible. Perhaps soon, I will do it all the time and on projects that pay well.

"Great women designers seem to have flourished in small practices often affiliated with art schools and universities or connected to publishing where the notion of self-generated work is not foreign or impractical. While this has become a matter of choice (especially for women designers with small children who want greater control of their time), it is also the result of the fact that women have not made strong inroads in the global corporate identity arena for Fortune 500 companies."

**Lucille Tenazas** (fig. 8.16)
Works in San Francisco, Calif.; principal, Tenazas Design, since 1985; professor affiliate of design, California College of Arts and Crafts, San Francisco, since 1985; clients include Apple Computer and Chronicle Books; projects for the public sector include San Francisco International Airport annual reports and information brochures and Port of San Francisco Draft Waterfront Land Use Plan.

"When I teach I talk about authorship which influences how I think in my own work. Traditionally the designer's voice has been relegated to the background. But the work would be empty if the soul of the designer weren't in it—I believe it's important to have the designer's voice heard. If you feel strongly about certain things, then they show in the work.

With my students I encourage them not to be afraid to make their work an extension of who they are and their critical views. Once you are self-aware, you can take projects proposed to you and not lose your voice.

"When I was a student I was told to be literal and clear, with no ambiguity, and serve the client. But to me that wasn't exciting. I started to entertain ambiguity, which opens the work up for the audience to participate. You have to assume intelligence on the part of the audience and the client.

"By multitasking I think of a wide range of tasks—professional, home, travel, school. Multitasking has traditionally been the domain of women, the strong suit of women, one of our skills, and it's been heightened in contemporary times so that even men are expected to do multitasking; these are hectic times. I'm from the Philippines originally and the whole concept of being as with it technologically as you can is not a part of me. I like to have technology around but not be ruled by it. I prac-

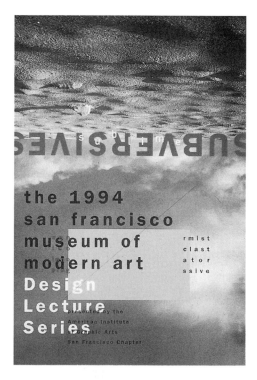

Lucille Tenazas, *Sublime Subversives,* postcard for a San Francisco Museum of Modern Art lecture series, 1994.
(8.16)

tice a holistic kind of multitasking—designing, teaching, being a mentor, mother, wife. I maintain a small office which is a version of family. I'm interested in working with like-minded people; I employ three to four people. My office is in a separate building next to my house. I'm 46 and have sons 2 and 5 years old—I can see them off and on throughout the day. My husband is a photographer, and his studio is in the basement of the house. I'm interested in a seamlessness of life and work and as far as work goes my priority is to do work I enjoy and believe in. Personal satisfaction tips it."

**Ann Tyler** (fig. 8.17)
Works in Chicago, Ill.; Ann Tyler Design, has had her own office since 1984; professor, The School of the Art Institute, Visual Communications department; exhibits at galleries, most recently, Betty Rymer Gallery, Chicago, 1999.

"I have always believed in the potential of design to raise questions and contribute to social dialogue. The requirements of full-time client-based work did not provide me the intellectual space needed for developing my

Ann Tyler, *It's No Different Than* (Chicago: Sara Ranchouse Publishing, 1999).
**(8.17)**

own work. Through a combination of teaching, client-based work, writing, and self-generated work I have the variety of intellectual stimulation that I need to produce my own work. There is also, of course, the issue of time. As my own work has developed, I have had the need to limit client-based work to projects that are of great interest to me and in some way contribute to the growth of my self-generated work. Financially this is possible because I teach full-time and because my financial goals do not focus on the most money I could make.

"My work examines issues of violence—particularly violence directed toward lesbians and gay men. These concerns arise for a number of different reasons, among them a sense of my own vulnerability. I produced a number of print works based on the murder of two lesbians in Oregon and during the course of my research read extensive interviews with their confessed murderer. Due to this focus I have done a lot of thinking about the human capacity for violence—small and large—and eventually became interested in working with the texts and visions of the murderer himself. This resulted in the book *It's No Different Than* and continues in a new series of prints currently in progress."


**Peggy Weil** (fig. 8.18)
Works in Los Angeles, Calif.; creator of new-media projects including *The Blurring Test—Convince Your Computer You Are Human*, 1998, a Web site funded by PBS/Weblab, *Moving Puzzle*, 1997–98, a series of eight CD-ROM puzzles published by Ravensburger, and *A Silly, Noisy House*, 1991, a CD-ROM for children published by the Voyager Company.

"When possible, I try to achieve the balance between work for clients and work for myself within the work itself.

"*A Silly Noisy House* (Voyager 1991) was for a client, but became very personal. Actually, it was somewhat self-generated because I'd approached Voyager several times throughout the eighties wanting to make an interactive laser disc. When CD-ROMs became a reality, Voyager came back and asked me to do a product, stipulating that it should be for children. From there I was free to invent a whole new structure based on my observations of my own kids.

"*The Blurring Test—Convince Your Computer You Are Human* is as self-inventing as self-generated. The project doesn't exist within any current definitions of product or art—it's a Chatterbot (a conversational software program) named MRMIND who, in an inversion of the Turing Test, challenges visitors to his Web site to convince him that they are human. I say self-inventing because it has taken on a life of its own. It's a Web site, it's a fictional character created by software, it's interactive fiction, or, maybe, nonfiction (these are real conversations).

"I can't use the term 'multitasking' in the context of work without discussing work and family and schools. I work at home so I'm constantly juggling public and private; motherwork and client/art work. FedEx and the Internet have made it possible for me to have a partner in San

Peggy Weil, *MRMIND,* 1999, from *The Blurring Test—Convince Your Computer You Are Human,* a Web site funded by PBS/Weblab and begun in 1998, <http://www.mrmind.com/mrmind>.
**(8.18)**

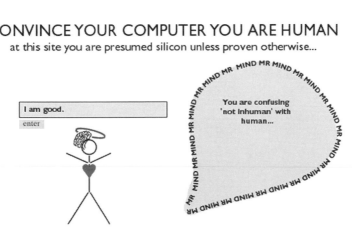

## CONVINCE YOUR COMPUTER YOU ARE HUMAN
at this site you are presumed silicon unless proven otherwise...

Francisco and a publisher in Germany, another producer in New York. To me, multitasking means finding a way to work creatively in short bursts tolerating frequent interruptions because of the number of diverse demands on my attention."

**Lorraine Wild** (fig. 8.19)
Works in Los Angeles, Calif.; principal, Lorraine Wild Graphic Design; former partner, 1991–96 in ReVerb; has been teaching design at the California Institute of the Arts since 1985; has designed over sixty-five books, recent projects have included exhibition catalogs for the Whitney Museum of American Art and the Museum of Contemporary Art in Los Angeles; writes frequently on design for publications including *Emigre, I.D.,* and *Graphic Design in America.*

"Everything about the way that I have been working for the last four years is about control, over the projects that I get to work on and the level of quality that I get to maintain in doing them. I deliberately have made a very

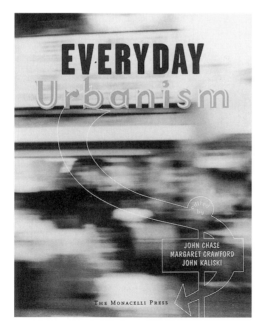

Lorraine Wild, cover; Lorraine Wild; Snow Kahn, Ninotchka Regets, and Amanda Washburn, book designers, *Everyday Urbanism,* ed. Margaret Crawford, John Chase, and John Kaliski (New York: The Monacelli Press, 1999); photograph: Dennis Keeley.
**(8.19)**

small practice (I work with one other designer, sometimes two) to keep overhead down in order to be able to do book design. The fees are not large, but I can still make the practice work financially if I keep it efficient. I enjoy book design because (1) I love reading, (2) I love the "object-ness" of books, and (3) I like to work on things that are relatively permanent, where there is a real record of the work that I do. A lot of other products that graphic designers create are quite temporal, and I've always found that a bit frustrating. The fact that book design is not that remunerative means that I have to be quite careful about the projects that I choose to work on. They have to be about subjects that I think are interesting because books do take a large amount of time and as I get older, I think one has to be careful about what you choose to give large chunks of your life over to!

"The work that I do in books is characterized by a very careful but engaged approach to the relationship between the conceptual content of the book and the form that I give to the book. I work very closely with editors, curators, artists, architects, and publishers to create books that are absolutely unique to their ideas. This is fairly difficult in some genres—like exhibition catalogs, for instance—where the sequence of essays, plates, and back matter are pretty well set. But it is precisely that problem that makes it interesting. I also work closely on the physical aspects of the book as well. I look at myself as being a very subtle visual translator of other people's content, but the product of my work is to make the ideas more vivid, more clear, more accessible, and more visually seductive, so it is satisfying to me in the end; it is my art, even though almost no one else perceives it as such.

"The other thing, of course, is that I write, and for the last few years the focus of my writing is to 'bear witness' so to speak to the changes in practice and teaching that have been accelerating in the last decade. I'm writing for the long term because I know that one of the strange difficulties about design history is that very few designers leave a record of what they are thinking. So I decided to record the changes as I saw them in the hopes that they are useful sometime in the future, since one thing I'm quite sure is that when people look back on the nineties they will realize that it was the time when everything about the practice of design was destabilized from what had been considered good and sure in the decades before. . . .

"My problems with money are entirely self-inflicted. By not going into corporate practice, I have marginalized myself financially. And that's all there is to it. Younger designers should know that some kind of price is attached to making an independent path. The fact that we are now living through one of those moments of prosperity when money is an even bigger god than usual is a drag, but doesn't really seem to affect things one bit."

**Fo Wilson** (fig. 8.20a–d)
Works in San Francisco, Calif.; vice-president, director of design for Tendo Communications, previously a graphic designer with her own practice in New York City.

"I don't often do self-generated work. This project, *"Mama, I thought only black people were bad,"* happened when a photographer I had often hired asked me to help her on a project. The posters ended up on city streets in New York and Los Angeles. We thought anonymity would help people focus more on the message, which is why we chose to represent ourselves as the Negro Art Collective.

Fo Wilson, *"Mama, I thought only black people were bad,"* four posters created in collaboration with The Negro Art collective, 1994.
**(8.20a–d)**

"I came of age in the sixties and seventies and the poster always represented a way of expressing personal outrage to the larger society. Even though the poster may be primitive next to more sophisticated twentieth-century media, its graphic context still commands a certain degree of attention. It's real and communicative, one-on-one.

"I closed my practice in New York. I work part-time as vice-president, director of design for Tendo Communications, a new company in San Francisco that develops custom-published products on the Web and in print for corporations looking to enhance their relationships with their clients and customers. So far we have diverse clients in technology, insurance, home furnishings, and management consulting. With my other time, I am taking classes in furniture design and welding with the hope of developing a personal body of work."

**Notes**

1. AIGA, *Salary and Benefits Survey*, 1994.
2. Martha Scotford, "Who Are We? Where Are We Going? *AIGA in Chicago* (Spring 1993): 6.
3. Families and Work Institute, *Women:The New Providers*, 1995, 33. Whirlpool Foundation Study.
4. Marcelle Karp and Debbie Stoller, eds., *The BUST Guide to the New Girl Order* (New York: Penguin, 1999), xiv–xv.
5. Chris Pullman, "Sense and Census," *Critique* 16 (Summer 2000):54–61.

# A Baby and a Coat Hanger:

## Visual Propaganda in the U.S. Abortion Debate

A fetus floating in amniotic fluid. Tiny fetal feet dangled by a pair of adult hands. A mutilated, bloodied, aborted fetus with a misshapen head and a missing arm. A doctor gagged. A coat hanger, dripping red. A dead woman, naked, her body partially covered by a sheet. Since 1973 when the Supreme Court issued the *Roe v. Wade* decision making first-trimester abortion legal in the United States, the abortion debate has become increasingly visual. Using new technologies in fetal imagery like ultrasound sonograms, the right-to-life movement has expanded its propaganda, emphasizing design and photographs. The pro-choice movement has produced generally less dramatic and less effective images of pregnant women, happy planned families, and that icon of desperation, the coathanger.

Most often, the visualization of the abortion debate has made the polarized arguments narrower. The imagery and graphics have tended to focus the discussion on individual rights of the fetus or, to a lesser degree, the mother while prompting almost no consideration of pertinent social contexts. Pictures of aborted fetuses and the like do not often lead to discussions of issues such as the economics of raising a child or the mechanics of adoption. Omitted in the abortion debate's picture-heavy propaganda are thorough explorations of a range of problems from the domestic, such

9

as responsibilities for child-raising within the family, to the national, such as lack of social services for families in the United States, to the global, such as perspectives on birth control and population.

In our highly individualistic culture, propaganda and advertising usually emphasize personal choice whether it's choice among brands of shampoo, types of cars, or the slants of political candidates. In this case, the visual repetition of portraits of fetuses and to some extent mothers has worked to pin the abortion debate's issues tightly to individual rights. Furthermore, the reduction of the abortion debate to a choice between a fetus's rights and a mother's has far-reaching consequences that are actually harmful to women. The abortion controversy is probably the single most comprehensive, public, visible, and noisy debate on women's issues in the nation. Yet, ironically, the current status of the discourse—the telescoping-down to a war of a few images, mainly the pro-life helpless fetus versus the pro-choice helpless woman—effectively blocks full discussion of societal issues on women and children that require democratic debate and legislative action.

In order to create a broader public discourse, it is helpful to consider first how the narrowing has occurred and to look at how images have functioned on both sides of the abortion debate to further exclude context. Second, I also discuss some possibilities for using design, photography, and other imaging techniques more ambitiously to increase the social effectiveness of current debates. As a cultural critic, then, I'm exploring a generative role as well as a reactive one, imagining what is not visualized and what needs to be and how it might be, in addition to critiquing the visuals that already exist.

**Prehistory of the Image Wars**

In the decades leading up to the 1973 decision, media coverage of abortion was limited but tended to contain at least some contextual issues. Illegal abortion was widespread and opinion was divided about when it was appropriate or not; in some cases and in some localities, abortion was even legal. Before *Roe v. Wade*, a patchwork of local and state laws and regulations were in place. For example, in some states, a hospital committee could approve an abortion if the mother's life were in danger. Cultural his-

A Baby and a Coat Hanger

torian Celeste Condit reports that by 1971 as many as 600,000 legal abortions were performed in the United States each year as well as countless illegal ones.[1]

The fifties and sixties saw increased media coverage about the practice, particularly newspaper and magazine profiles of women having legal or illegal abortions. Unlike today, discussion in the press was not so much about the moral choices associated with abortion as it was about the fate of the women involved. Still, stereotypes reigned, but at least they had some dimension. The articles tended to portray women as powerless victims, either mistreated by back-alley abortionists or subject to invasive scrutiny by hospital boards and doctors. As Condit has argued, "for a broad public to feel sorry for the agent and angry with the forces that bring her suffering, the character depicted must be 'good' or, at the least, unable to control her own destiny."[2]

Most famous, and yet still typical as a story of a good mother deserving the choice to abort, was the 1962 case of Sherri Finkbine, host of the children's television program *Romper Room* in Phoenix, Arizona. Married and a mother of four, Finkbine was pregnant for the fifth time when she mistakenly took thalidomide contained in a tranquilizer. Later she learned that her child would have a 50 percent chance of having severe deformities, and she and her husband decided to abort the embryo. Her local hospital committee approved the abortion decision, despite the fact that Arizona state law permitted abortion only in the case of saving the mother's life. When Finkbine, before the operation, went public with her story to warn other mothers of the danger of thalidomide, the hospital balked, fearing legal suits. Running out of time, Finkbine went to Sweden for an abortion, and a deformed fetus was removed. Going by media accounts, it appears that the public continued to sympathize with her and see her as a "good" figure.

Although the focus of this story and many like it was still on individual choice and not—outside of arguments about legalization—on social context, at least there was discussion of the mother's life and the factors like number of children already born to the family that informed her decision.

## Rise of Fetal Imagery

In 1965, an important shift occurred in the types of images available to the abortion debate. *Life* magazine published the startling, entrancing, full-color images of the fetus at different growth stages by Swedish photographer Lennart Nilsson. Most of the now-classic photographs were taken of embryos and fetuses that had been surgically removed from the mother. However, the introductory image in the photo essay was "the first portrait ever made of a living embryo inside its mother's womb. . . . [U]sing a specially built super wide-angle lens and a tiny flash beam at the end of a surgical scope, Nilsson was able to shoot this picture of a living 15-week-old embryo, its eyes still sealed shut, from only one inch away."[3] To this day, the details of the photographs fascinate us with their intimacy: the framing of the red crystalline encasing of an eleven-week fetus or the view of a twenty-eight-week-old fetus veiled in its membrane. The spectacle is heightened by showing all the fetuses outside of or separate from the mother (the womb is invisible in the living embryo portrait). This visually dramatic technique has since been often reused with a different ideological slant in right-to-life propaganda. As historian Rosalind Petchesky and others have argued, when viewers become familiar with seeing the fetus independent of the mother, they can more easily begin to consider fetal rights as if separable from maternal ones.[4]

Ultrasound images of fetuses also became available in the 1960s and commonplace in the1970s—in everyday use and in propaganda. First introduced into obstetrical practice in the early 1960s, the procedure, used on pregnant women, is to create either a still image (scan) or a real-time moving image by bouncing sound waves off the fetus in the womb. By the mid-eighties, over one-third of all pregnant women in the United States were examined with ultrasound. To date, the most dramatic pro-life incorporation of ultrasound moving imagery is in *The Silent Scream*, the 1984 film showing a fetus in real time undergoing an abortion.

With the use of ultrasound images in abortion propaganda, as with close-up fetal photographs, anti-abortion activists developed their primary propaganda technique: showing the fetus without reference to the mother's body and thus depersonalizing the mother. She is not visible and certainly not portrayed as a person with a life history and an economic context. This technique has now become highly sophisticated. For example, in a recent National Right-to-Life Committee brochure, in an image reminiscent of one of Nilsson's photographs, a color photo of an enlarged fetus surrounded by placenta is shown on a black background. The accompanying text, addressing the reader as "you," deftly appeals to the reader to identify directly with the fetus while bypassing any consideration of the mother. The brochure takes us step by step through the fetal growth process and reads, at month three, "your movements became more energetic, less mechanical and more graceful and fluid, very much like an astronaut floating and enjoying his gravity-free space capsule. Your arms grew to be as long as printed exclamation marks and your fingers and toes quickly formed, complete with fingerprints which gave you a separate legal identity that would never change except for size."

This compelling propagandistic use of the fetus raises questions about why readers might identify so strongly with the image. To look at photographs of fetuses is to be stunned by the spectacle of human life unfolding and to be captivated, with pictures of more developed fetuses, by their babylike qualities. However, beyond this, the connotations of innocence and helplessness are used in pro-life literature in a particularly American way. The individual as the protagonist of persuasive literature is a typical device in U.S. culture. In addition, images of children, and especially fetuses, present an "innocent" individual whose origins are guilt- and blame-free, and who is deserving of care and help. Because we are a self-help, individualistic society rather than a cooperative, communally based one, it is perhaps only in this originary position that individuals are considered completely deserving of help. Right-to-life propaganda portrays the fetus as a human being at its origin and (seen in close-up) seemingly without ties and without support. The importance of individual identity for our culture could relate directly to our deep identification with fetal imagery. Anthropologist Faye Ginsburg has argued the appeal, in this context, of "the American charter myth of 'starting over' . . . the metaphor of being 'born again' (or its secular version of 'free choice')."[5] The unmoored fetus, then, functions as a symbol of innocence, of the frontier, and of the open road of choice—of birth and rebirth, of an individual beholden to no one, especially to his or her mother, and yet deserving of protection from everyone.

**Graphics that Expand the Debate**

Altogether, a visual abortion-debate forum currently exists in which the polemical print graphics of the National Right-to-Life Committee are hard hitting but focus primarily on issues of individual rights, and Planned Parenthood's milder print propaganda usually centers on individual women and families. (There are some instructive exceptions, however, in the Planned Parenthood literature that do address social context.) Is it possible to imagine or find examples of visual propaganda that link personal decisions to societal context and group political action? Why is there a near-total silence in the debate on alternatives to abortion such as birth control and adoption and on the national social issues surrounding the economic pressures of raising children? Currently, there is even silence about women's issues within the area of individual choice: about how reproductive decisions play out over a woman's life cycle and trigger conflicts between survival and nurturing, between marketplace and domestic definitions of what it means to be an adult woman.

In a muted way, though, Planned Parenthood has occasionally given some of these questions thought and even pictures. For example, their literature and their programs have consistently promoted the use of birth control and expanded birth-control research. A well-argued piece of propaganda (a glossy one-page handout produced during the Bush years) is punctuated on the top and bottom with white-on-black callouts: NOTES FOR A NEW ADMINISTRATION / A KINDER, GENTLER NATION BEGINS WITH FAMILY PLANNING. Presented in a tabloidlike layout, the text announcing "federal funding for contraceptive R & D has declined 25%—in real dollars—over the past decade" is headlined "If you have a complaint about your birth control, here's where to send it" and illustrated with a photograph of the White House. Still, none of Planned Parenthood's images to date have the comprehensive, ad-campaign-star charisma of the fetus featured in pro-life imagery. A call for government-

A Baby and a Coat Hanger

funded preventive social services is crucial, but it doesn't quite have the drama of life-and-death abortion choices.

Complex issues, even the urgent ones, can be difficult to translate into images. Particularly slippery is the whole issue of victimhood when it's a status claimed for the mother. As Condit has noted, the spotlight is on the innocent victim in the abortion debates. But if the "victim" is portrayed as too pathetic, identification breaks down—if represented as too strong and independent, then (in our hyperindividualistic culture) undeserving of help. Images of grown women are tricky in this regard. One Planned Parenthood handout negotiates stereotypes of independence and victimhood with a two-thirds-page melodramatic photograph—caption superimposed, "How would you like the police to investigate your miscarriage?"—of a white, middle-class woman opening the door of her home to two plainclothes policemen. She is the victim of an invasion of privacy: An analogy is established between police intruding into her home and the government potentially threatening her freedom of choice. The picture of this invasive fantasy, though, has none of the impact or biological realism of images of a growing fetus.

In the same newspaper-format series of one-page handouts is "Poverty doesn't come cheap." It illustrates a photo of a healthy but ragged child leaning out of a glassless window from inside a ghastly apartment. The text makes a multilayered plea for sympathy for children who are victims of poverty and for empathy with parents trapped in poverty by unintended pregnancy—and also to taxpayers' self-interest by demonstrating how much unplanned pregnancies cost. But the healthy little boy in the photo looks as if he's doing alright despite all odds. Planned Parenthood has avoided producing yet another overly pathetic image of a poor person (the common, dehumanizing stereotype), but offers instead a boy surprisingly untouched by circumstances.

The solutions to large questions of how we in the United States appeal to each other for help and mobilize for social change go beyond questions of individual graphics. In the abortion debates, the foregrounded issues are the sanctity of life, rights of the fetus and the mother, tensions between personal privacy and government regulations, and the American sense of entitlement to individual choice. In the broadest sense, the unspoken background questions revolve around how we conceive our identities as citizens—banded together and/or individualistic and competitive. If, as Americans, we could ever reconceive our concept of group responsibility then we wouldn't need to portray people as victims in order to argue they deserve help. A vision of interdependence among adults, a true community of citizens, is lacking in U.S. popular culture—and sorely needed as a motivating dream.

Meanwhile, within the individualistic culture we've inherited, what alternatives to mainstream abortion graphics could be effective? The challenge is to connect portrayals of individuals (the mother, the fetus) to broader contexts, ones that move the discussion toward social change in conjunction with individual choice and responsibility. Perhaps we do need to be motivated by identifying with individuals, but that doesn't mean that our emotional investment in a given issue needs to be restricted to that. Images and propaganda can prompt fuller fantasies of a dual identification, with both an individual and a community, and also a creative sense of the interconnectedness between people. In some cases, such propaganda already exists; in others, it is to be imagined.

As positive examples, some activist artists and designers have produced work that lobbies for abortion rights and also raises issues about women's self-images. Some artists have raised identity issues in graphics primarily created in response to immediate political situations—Barbara Kruger with her pro-choice imagery (fig. 9.1), Bethany Johns and Georgie Stout for WAC (Women's Action Coalition), and Marlene McCarty and Donald Moffett with their design students at Yale. Kruger's pro-choice poster *Your body is a battleground* designed for a 1989 march on Washington presents a photograph of a woman divided into positive and negative halves. Characteristic of Kruger, the photomontage points to the use of women's images in the pull of mass culture's seductions; Johns and Stout's poster, also created for a pro-choice march on Washington in 1992, uses the printed image of Durer's praying hands with the caption "Pray for Choice" to recapture the claim of morality for the pro-choice side (fig. 9.2). Although these two works, *Your body is a battleground* and *Pray* for *Choice* are aesthetically sophisticated in their use of appropriation and recontextualizing compositions, effective activist designs need not be aesthetically innovative. Some, instead, may even mimic a sober, governmental look—that is, "plain-speaking" design—as with the stark, text-only pro-choice billboard created by McCarty and Moffett's students. The Yale students dealt with the issues of silence and shame by painting a billboard (1992, the spring before the Clinton-Bush presidential election) outside New Haven simply with black letters over a solid yellow ground stating "73% of America is pro-choice: Why doesn't it seem that way?" The next year, in 1993, McCarty and Moffett's students formed the Coalition to Free RU-486 and created a media kit for television talk

Barbara Kruger, *Your body is a battleground,* poster image, 1989.
(**9.1**)

Bethany Johns and Georgie Stout, *Pray for Choice,* poster image, 1992.
(**9.2**)

shows that was distributed to Oprah, Donahue, and ten others. It contained the usual press gimmicks like a T-shirt stating "I want my RU-486," but also information on legalization, biographies of potential talk show guests on both sides of the issues, and factual information about the drug's use in abortion and other medical procedures. Significantly, these designers were not restricted to formal concerns, but rather took responsibility for content and research and strove to manipulate the media, not just produce for it.

In 1994, the New York–based Population Council obtained the rights to the medical abortion pill RU-486, and in 2000 after FDA review, RU-486 (mifepristone) became available publicly in the United States. However, even with the sale of RU-486 in the United States, the visual face of the debate is not likely to change much. The administration of RU-486 is still dependent on visits to doctors. Individual women are likely to be harassed less; medical abortion is less traceable because any kind of doctor can prescribe it, and women don't have to go to abortion clinics or even ob-gyns. But anti-abortion forces still of course object to medical abortions on moral grounds and can target manufacturers and suppliers that make RU-486 available. And it's not cheap—funding for poor women is still a problem.

It's also possible to look outside the abortion debate for effective visual propaganda that deals with issues of reproduction. The global threat of overpopulation—another issue that you would think would be at the center of reproductive debates but is missing—can be found in the heated arguments around wildlife conservation. The literature of the World Wildlife Fund at least acknowledges the conflicts in developing countries between rapidly growing human populations and natural resources. Artists, designers, and writers working in conservation and environmental areas have addressed the dangers of overpopulation. Exotically different but intimately connected to man's reproductive debates, for example, is the powerful propaganda warning about the suffering caused by animal overpopulation in Peter Beard's text and photo book *End of the Game* about wildlife mismanagement, overpopulation, and the ultimate starvation of over 30,000 elephants in Kenya's Tsavo National

Park.[6] In his photographs, Beard captured images of dead elephants slammed against rutted earth, dropped while running, exhausted while burrowing into the earth for water, or starved while gnawing desperately through baobab trees.

It's quite odd though that the most effective visual propaganda about overpopulation exists in cultural pockets outside the human reproductive context. Controlling the population surge, in fact, has become a non-subject in the United States. According to the liberal lobbying group the Communications Consortium, which has run focus groups on attitudes toward overpopulation, most people here see it as a global but not a national problem, as if the two are separable. And, for some, the eugenics connotations of involving public debate, public consensus, and government in this issue are uncomfortable. While in the late 1960s and early 1970s, the goal of zero population growth and the dangers of overpopulation were very much part of public discussions, today, although staggering population growth and starvation have continued unabated—we keep reproducing and denying that we lack resources to feed everyone— little mass-culture discourse exists on overpopulation. The focus of our reproductive debates instead remains solely on the mechanics of abortion, moral choices, and individual rights.

**Conclusion**

Today we have an abortion debate that's stuck. Dominated by fetal imagery, it talks about sanctity of life and personal choice without any broad discussion of our societal conditions of life and the hard-pressing factors that make up the choice of whether or not to bear a child. Although pro-life literature, more than pro-choice, veers away from any government intervention, both sides downplay societywide responsibilities for raising the next generation. We need to expand the debate to get to the real issues that define how people make their difficult public and private choices and to examine how to consider these choices as individual and/or perhaps community based.

So, how can we change the debate and democratically open it up to issues that desperately need widespread discussion like the lack of social services in the United States that help, in other countries, with the expense of raising a child? Can we imagine visual propaganda about reproductive rights that also proselytizes for a more generous vision of citizenship and mutual responsibility? Concretely, in my view, we need to discuss and to create visual propaganda about the following issues—family allowances, adoption, health care for families of all classes, caring for children with disabilities, enforcement of child-care payments, and equal pay for women. These are key reproductive-rights issues that inform the choice of whether or not to carry a pregnancy to term. On the most basic level, we need to acknowledge the relationship between giving birth and raising a child, and we need to fully accept government and community, as well as individual and familial responsibility for the next generation of citizens—a goal we need not be distracted from by magnified photos of the free-floating spaceman fetus and images created in reaction to him.

Ironically, or perhaps not, one of the few community-oriented pieces of propaganda created in the context of the abortion debate is a 1994 TV ad funded by the right-wing De Moss Foundation in the series "Life—What a Beautiful Choice" produced in conjunction with the National Right-to-Life Committee. It shows a rainbow group of inner-city children in school uniforms sitting on school steps. While the voice-over preaches against abortion, the visual image is one of equal opportunity and an implication of quality services well provided. It gives a societal vision of fairness for the next generation that is unfortunately far from the truth—and that gap is what begs for more discussion.

**Notes**

1. Celeste Condit, *Decoding Abortion Rhetoric: Communicating Social Change* (Urbana: University of Illinois Press, 1990): 22.
2. Condit, *Decoding Abortion Rhetoric*, 25.
3. "Drama of Life Before Birth," photographed by Lennart Nilsson, *Life* (30 April 1965): 54–67.
4. Rosalind Petchesky, "Fetal Images: The Power of Visual Culture in the Politics of Reproduction," *Feminist Studies* (Summer 1987): 263–292.
5. Faye Ginsburg, *Contested Lives: The Abortion Debate in an American Community* (Berkeley: University of California Press, 1989): 220–21.
6. Peter Beard, *End of the Game* (San Francisco: Chronicle Books, 1988 [1963]).

A Baby and a Coat Hanger

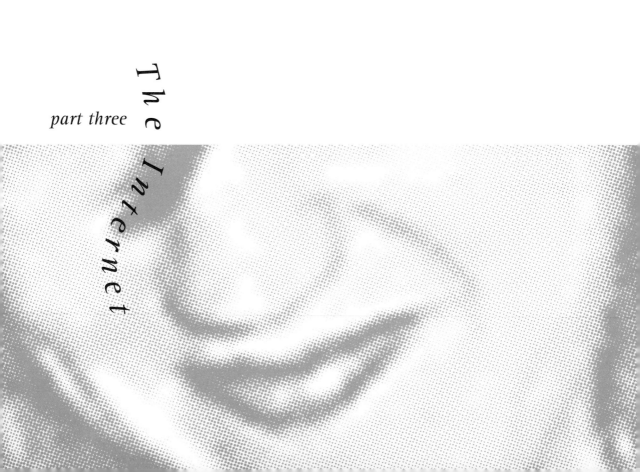

part three

The Internet

# Dirty Work and Clean Faces:

## The Look of Intelligent Agents on the Internet

Ideas about intelligent agents contain the electronic world's dearest fantasies and darkest fears about duplicating human behavior. But, the practical reality is that agents operating now on the Internet are not all that sophisticated. Instead, existing agents are somewhat clunky versions of much more elaborate ones imagined for the future.

Conceptually, agents are programs that learn your habits and interests as you use the computer (on its own and/or within a network). Based on this capsule portrait of you, agents then operate, with some degree of independence, to fetch news items, do research, sort e-mail, pay bills, and even shop. They can represent you as your avatar. The agent's graphical interface or user interface is the collection of images and words on your computer screen telling you what the agent is doing and showing you what the agent has brought you. Mechanisms in use now that help you do research on the Internet—such as Yahoo!, which searches the World Wide Web using keywords you provide—can be considered rudimentary agents. But these lack the exciting or sinister (depending on your point of view) capacity to monitor and study your habits on the computer. Prototypes for this kind of software behavior do exist, though, at MIT's Media Lab and elsewhere, agents that watch you in order to assist you, even comparing what they learn with agents of your co-workers to increase their body of knowledge. In the future, the spread of agents on the Net seems assured because they save time, labor, and money. Efficient as they may be, though, agents raise questions about privacy, control, and communication, questions that trigger hopes and anxieties about the future of the Internet.

I talked about these issues with Pattie Maes, Associate Professor at the Media Lab, who is developing software agents. Some of her agents like an e-mail sorter sound straightforward and similar to ones in commercial use now (the Qualcom company's Eudora, for example, is a popular and easily programmable e-mail sorter in common use). Others are more ambitious and raise complex questions. Maes sees her programs as service-oriented. You delegate some responsibilities, and an agent does your dirty work for you. In conversation, she offers the analogy of a personal assistant. And in her writings, Maes describes matter-of-factly the mundane operations of various agents, like a "news filtering" one that brings a user newspaper articles on topics the agent knows the user is already interested in: "the interface agent learns by continually 'looking over the shoulder' of the user as the user is performing actions. The interface agent can monitor the activities of the user, keep track of all of his or her actions over long periods of time (weeks or months), find regularities and recurrent patterns and offer to automate these. . . . [I]f a news filtering agent detects some patterns in the articles the user reads, then it can offer similar articles to the user when it discovers them."[1] On the one hand, I can see how a news filtering agent could be useful. When I was working on this chapter, it would have helped to log onto the Net every morning and see what new articles my agent had brought me about intelligent agents and user interfaces. This wouldn't have stopped me from, in addition, doing my own research, although if I were feeling particularly lazy or pressed for time, it might have. Nor would it have been a serious invasion of privacy: the agent would have simply been using workaday information, probably even information I'd given it, to perform a workaday service for me.

On the other hand, some problems are immediately obvious. Agents can serve up research in a way that's limiting. They're about going to where the user has already gone instead of stumbling—accidentally and creatively—into new territory. The danger is in feeding the already familiar to the already interested, constructing, as "cybrarian" Reva Bausch has put it, computer users as a bunch of "dittoheads."[2] As it turns out, some of the most helpful and creative research I did for this essay was accidental in its sources. For instance, I talked to Ron MacNeil at the MIT Media Lab's Visible Language Workshop (formerly run by Muriel Cooper). Agent graphics and software design were not his specialty; the person I really needed to reach, and eventually did, was Henry Lieberman. But, in the meantime, MacNeil and I had a fascinating talk about a layered approach to knowing what exactly an agent is doing and how to show this graphically. And I learned a lot from Peggy Weil, an interactive media artist, again not an agent expert, who is interested in fictions we have about duplicating ourselves and our learning systems on the computer. My news filtering agent would not have brought me articles by MacNeil and Weil; I reached them through human chains of conversation, essentially through telephone networking.

The biggest potential problem with agents, though, is loss of privacy. Agents are monitoring systems. As a friend of mine is fond of saying, an expression that seems apt when discussing all this monitoring, "There's no such thing as paranoia." Some businesses, such as Time Warner, have already been criticized for checking their employees' hard drives to make sure company computers are being used only for company work. Agents "looking over your shoulder" will only make this kind of invasion easier. Privacy issues will be compounded by "multiagent collaboration," which already exists in prototype use. It means your agent will confer and compare notes with other agents. As Maes explains, "When the agent does not have enough confidence in its prediction. . . , it asks for help from other agents. . . . The agent sends part of the description of the situation to other agents via e-mail and awaits their response. . . . The agent will make a prediction based on the different suggestions that are returned. . . . The multiagent communication is an excellent method for transfer of information and competence among different users in a workgroup."[3] So how do we protect our privacy?

We need to control agents instead of being controlled by them, and this is where good graphical and software interface design comes in. Like it or not, the consensus in the electronic world is that we will come increasingly to use agents to filter information and perform tasks. If so, there will be a pressing need to know what agents are doing, how they're doing it, what other agents they're conversing with, and what their limits are. Users need to have input, control, and knowledge. The graphical interface is where it will or won't happen—where this essential knowledge will or won't be visible. After all, it's at the surface level of the interface—the images on the computer screen—that the user is informed of the agent's doings and can tell the agent what to do. We need software and interfaces designed so that the everyday user can control an agent's searching and monitoring. And, conversely, we need interfaces that remind the user of the limits of the agent and so encourage the user to go beyond an agent's operations when exploring information and its contexts.

To start at the most basic level, what the agent's face looks like can suggest both the agent's limits and potentials. Maes uses cartoonlike caricatured faces for her agent prototypes so they don't seem too smart. She explained to me, "The issue of anthropomorphization has been discussed a lot in the user interface community. There was a 'Guides' video from Apple about user interfaces of the future and they used video of human faces talking natural language. This was criticized as giving the user incorrect expectations about the intelligence level of the agent." Maes's team uses abstracted facial expressions to clue in the user to what the agent is doing—a confused expression, for instance, means the agent needs more instruction.

Jaron Lanier, musician, computer scientist, and inventor of the concept of virtual reality, has written against the development of agents, objecting to our ceding autonomy to, as he puts it, small, reduced portraits of ourselves that could run tirelessly around the Net rooting truffles. "They are a powerful fantasy," said Lanier when I interviewed him. "An imaginary way you don't have to die if consciousness doesn't have to be in a body." Accordingly Lanier argues against this living entity model of agent graphics, "By the act of thinking of something as an agent you project behavior onto it, like a pet. People have to reduce themselves to work with agents. For agents to become part of your method, they become an external thing that you can have make decisions for you. You become passive." Lanier implies what agent graphics should look like when he says, "Agents should be reconstituted as search/query tools. They'll become more useful and whatever they do or don't do will be laid bare."[4]

In contrast, Susan Kare, a leading computer interface graphic designer, feels that an abstract face is fitting precisely because the user can project herself onto it and think of the agent as an extension of herself. Kare, interviewed in 1995 when she was at the software company General Magic, was one of the pioneers in designing Macintosh reality-metaphor icons like the trash can and the paintbrush. I asked her whether interface graphics could also signal the limits of an agent's capacities. "Well, I'm not sure that should be done graphically," she answered, opting instead for quick legibility. "After all, there's a reason we don't still use hieroglyphs."

Are these arguments about the look of agents nitpicking? I don't think so. In the choices we have about how we'll use agents—whether agents will constrict our creativity or free us from information overload or influence us further to be obedient consumers—graphics will play an important role. I'm interested, for example, in how an effective graphical interface could counter the limiting aspects of agents on research. While I was researching this chapter, I often thought of the analogy between how computer users can come to rely on agents and how I've come to use open-stack libraries. Even when a library has open stacks, I rarely wander through them, relying instead on computerized search mechanisms that point me to specific sources for which I then make a beeline. And yet I'm a firm believer in browsing as a key component of creative research. This loss of free-form exploring in favor of computerized searches is an even greater problem on the Net. Even sophisticated information-search mechanisms like Architext, software brainstormed by a group of Stanford grads that searches by related concepts it finds in documents as well as by keywords, lacks the rambling curiosity of a human researcher.

I talked to Ron MacNeil of the MIT Media Lab's Visible Language Workshop about what it means to browse on the Net and how you could foster browsing with agents. MacNeil suggests you could "open the hood, look behind the scenes" to understand what an agent is and isn't doing so you could go beyond it. This desire, in turn, links the agent interface discussion to the old clarity versus complexity debates in computer graphics. Computer graphics are, in a sense, MacNeil asserts, all about "managing visual complexity, maintaining clarity and focus." Similarly, programming software interfaces focuses on reduced and cleaned-up communication. Along these lines, Maes says bluntly, "an agent is a way of hiding complexity. For some operations like mail sorting, they're so boring you don't care how they work." But for other operations such as research, it can be crucial to know the path an agent has traveled. MacNeil imagines, "When we have more bandwidth we could let the user choose how close to get to the info, and the closer you get the more context would be visible." Words and graphics could also be employed to remind the user to go beyond the limits of the agent's operations.

Context is all important for issues of power and communication on the Net. Without clear signals as to the context of a piece of information, it's hard to interpret it. At present most information gleaned from the Net—whether delivered by a search mechanism and/or the user's own browsing on various Web sites—tends to look disconcertingly alike, often with the deceptive feel of raw data as if it is unauthored and without point of view, or all from similar points of view. This apparent sameness discourages a knowing interpretation on the part of the user, in contrast to what happens currently with print media. When I pick up a copy of the *The New York Post*, a conservative tabloid, I know the political orientation I'm getting. But when I use the Yahoo! index to search under the keywords "Newt Gingrich," I get a lot of material making fun of the former Speaker mixed in with information about his speeches. I find this humorous, but there are other occasions when the lack of authorship and context is confusing. In some cases it goes beyond encouraging an unsuspecting user to swallow information whole to intentional manipulation as in the stock selling scams on the Net. With agents bringing users material, the potential exists for another layer further decontextualizing the information, obscuring the authorship, and clouding the point of view. Graphics could inform users about the sources of information that agents deliver.

Agents are essentially filters. Inevitably this raises questions about who owns the filters. Who influences them? Won't they themselves have points of view according to who programs them? Who profits from them? As the Internet becomes more commercial, agents will do more shopping. Already with existing shopping software, a user can graphically travel from his desk, down a hallway, "outside" to downtown, and into a building to buy airline tickets. The user inputs basic information like destination, time, credit card number, and cost limits, and the agent does comparative shopping and purchases the tickets. One theory about the future of advertising on the Net is that it will have to make an effort to attract agents, for example, to lure agents to a Web site.

I spoke with Jake Prescott, Creative Technology Director at the advertising firm Ogilvy and Mather, when he was working on, among other things, constructing IBM's brand presence on the company's Web site. I asked him about the idea of using popular keywords ("sex" is a big one) to attract search mechanisms and eventually agents to a site. "Whatever attracts people will attract agents. If the agents are any good, they'll be programmed by the people who use them. If you trick them—the user or the agent—they'll never come back to the site again." He continued, "If electronic advertising is too controlled or controlling, it goes against the grain of what people like about the Net in the first place and how they feel while they're on it—flexible, adaptable, ingenuous, alert." He sees effective advertising on the Net for now as providing a service or information for free and then advertising, at least with a brand, on the relevant pages. How this practice might change with a heavier reliance on agents, whether agents will do a great volume of shopping, whether agents can be programmed to strip ads off information, whether shopping agents can be manipulated by hackers for theft, remains to be seen.

The concern, though, that as agents get more active, users will get more passive is already pertinent and needs to be addressed, I would argue, at the level of the graphical interface. Another MIT prototype agent, this one an entertainment agent with great potential for both amusement and sales, exists. Formerly called "Ringo," now "Firefly" (for trademark reasons), this "social filtering" program asks the user what kinds of music he or she likes and then makes recommendations about what new CDs fit his or her taste. It's all done by comparing the user to other user profiles and extrapolating from other people's taste. For instance, I like classics by Janis Joplin and Patti Smith and, in terms of newer sounds, the girl group Veruca Salt. Three completely different kinds of music, with provocative female lyrics and confident, albeit unlike, styles. So if Firefly heard from someone else who is interested in Joplin and Smith, it would match her taste to mine (and others) and perhaps recommend Veruca Salt to her. Users have reported being surprised by how accurate Firefly can be in predicting even the most seemingly oddball leaps in preferences. It's fun for the user; you could see how it could be profitable too for music companies. But in early testing situations the Media Lab discovered a problem. Users tended to log on for Firefly's suggestions but were lazy about feeding it new information, information Firefly needed to update its database to continue to be effective. The agent story is all there: the user's leaning toward dependency, the obvious need for graphics to remind the user that Firefly has limits and needs human input. And what about the user's needs? Maybe on one level, the user just wants some music suggestions. On another level, it's entertaining in a kind of narcissistic way to have the computer guess your preferences. But on yet another level, one that's missing so far, the user might also want to know more about how Firefly works and what Firefly is doing and to whom Firefly is comparing him or her. This knowledge too can be just for entertainment. It can just teach the user more about how "social filtering agents" work. Significantly, more knowledge could also protect the user, in the future, from being manipulated by a record company or whoever is trying to make a profit off her. (Over time, Firefly's capacities have expanded; it now can demand privacy policy info from each Web site a user visits as well as collect a range of information about the user. In April 1998 Microsoft bought Firefly and touted it as "a major step forward for personal privacy," *The New York Times* reported. Privacy advocate David Sobel countered, if privacy is the issue "why is the emphasis on collecting data at all?")

In terms of the current and potential commercialization of the Net, agents are more likely to weigh in on the corporation's side than the user's. There's a real possibility of the user's privacy being invaded to garner information for profit, particularly by computer companies. In fact, in the summer of 1995 when Microsoft introduced Windows 95 accompanied by operatic publicity, a rumor circulated that it included, along with its network capabilities, automatic monitoring of everything on the user's hard drive. The point was supposed to be that Microsoft would use this information both to capture software pirates and to gauge user habits for the creation of future products. The rumor ran so rapidly and broadly that it was even reported—and denied by Microsoft—on the front page of *The Wall Street Journal*. The rumor may indeed have been false, but the fear was real.

The way to counteract the loss of power created by privacy-invading agents is to know what agents are doing—and for the user to have programming control. There's no doubt, in the case of agents, knowledge is power. And computer graphics can communicate that knowledge in a condensed and effective way. Right now, agents present us with clean faces as they do our dirty work. In the future, we need to see some more of that dirt on the screen.

**Notes**

1. Pattie Maes, "Agents that Reduce Work and Information Overload," *Communications of the ACM* 37, no. 7 (July 1994): 33.
2. R. B., interviewed by John Whalen, *Wired* (May 1995): 153.
3. Maes, "Agents that Reduce Work and Information Overload," 37.
4. See also J. L., "Agents of Alienation," *Journal of Consciousness Studies* 2, no. 1 (Oxford) (1995): 76–81.

# Confessions from *The Couch:*

## Issues of Persona on the Web

For a year and a half, I wrote a character named Celeste in a cyberdrama called *The Couch*, a semi-serious soap opera for the Web, created by myself and seven other writers (fig. 11.1). We played and wrote fictionalized versions of ourselves as eight New Yorkers in group therapy. The content consisted of text, graphics, and photographs of therapy sessions, private diaries, and side episodes. We wrote for almost a year together before we went public on the Web as <http://www.thecouch.com>, so we launched with a hefty backlog. Then we put up new material every day for twenty-six weeks, roughly the first half of 1997. This twenty-six-week season stands as a work on its own, like a three-dimensional novel, with each character completing a trajectory, and interweaving plots reaching satisfying developments, if not closure.

Some of the most popular locations on the Web, outside of those selling sex and sports paraphernalia, are diaristic and interactive, and we were no exception. We received over 10,000 visitors a day at our peak, and lively regulars participated in our interactive component (which is now inactive and the rest of the site is on pause; the entire site is still visible and visitable, we're just not putting up new material). The interactive part was called "Transference." Unlike most diaristic Web sites, we were edited by one of the writers, Adam Penenberg, and we put our texts through many drafts. We paid great

11

David Steuer, designer, screen grab from *The Couch*, 1997.
**(11.1)**

attention to the writing, with some enticing results. So we got a lot of play in the press both in the print world—*The New York Times, The New York Daily News, Entertainment Weekly, Time Out*—and online—*The Atlantic Monthly, People, The New York Times* again, Yahoo!, Netscape, and from other sites that hyperlinked with us like the Nunbun site.

At first I thought this writing experience would be wildly different from the writing I'd done as an art historian and scholar, in *Cut with the Kitchen Knife* on Hannah Höch's 1920s photomontages or even from my contemporary articles on photography and design. Stylistically, it was. But there were also continuities. One continuing thread, I see now in retrospect, was my interest in montage and the ambiguities of identity it could represent. Höch's photomontages, and even more so John Heartfield's, for all their ambiguity, do involve the reader in an evolutionary process of forming meaning. Still, it's a somewhat passive role for the reader. In electronic media today though, whether someone is downloading images and manipulating them with Photoshop or just surfing the Web and chatting, a more active role is possible in forming and experiencing montage and montage identities. So, writing for *The Couch* for me was like an Alice in Wonderland drop from the surface of montage to the layers underneath, from observing 1920s montages and their historical ripples to creating a montage identity in flux and in dialogue with other producers. In particular, I made some discoveries about persona issues on the Web, about leading a semi-fictionalized life of ambiguous identity formation, neither completely fluid nor completely mimetic—a montage.

"Persona," in a Jungian sense, is the personality an individual presents to the world, a set of attitudes adopted by an individual to fit himself or herself for a social role or roles. The idea of multiplicity is important here: every social person is a collection of roles. Subsequently, authenticity is disputed—questions abound regarding whether or how these social attitudes are connected to the inner self, drives, desires, needs, identity. Do these masks alienate us from our feelings and needs, or do they pragmatically help to feed them? For me one of the most useful questions is do we have self-awareness about how we use these masks? I don't see a pure self as somehow operating independently from a socially derived persona; rather, I see these layers of identity as interdependent, although psychologically I think it's helpful to have some kind of working map. Even in Jung's schematic thinking, the persona is described as a kind of "compromise between an individual and society as to what a man should appear to be."[1] Therapy, and not only Jungian therapy, enters in here, as does popular culture, and in the case of *The Couch*, popular culture inflected in form and content by psychotherapies. However different, many therapies deal with the relationships between what we present of ourselves and what we feel. I'm not looking, though, for only therapeutic motivations in exploring personae, but at play and transformation in the creative representation of personae on the Web. I'm interested in personae as they function in representation more than in therapeutic healing.

The word *persona* cannot be defined only in terms of therapies and popular culture. There is an economy to its functions as well, and the cultural and the economic functions of course overlap. The social personality in U.S. culture is also so often a commodified, marketed mask or collection of roles. To cite a prominent example in the art world, Andy Warhol used his Factory to manufacture his public and saleable identity as much as to produce artworks and to enhance a social scene. Dennis Hopper's photographs of the Factory emphasize the drugged masks formed by the faces of the people who hung out there. Today we are extremely knowing about the displays of marketable personae in popular culture; music videos, in particular, often promote a planned obsolescence of personae, always new, always changing.

For noncelebrities, the world of therapy can lend itself to an awareness of marketing personae, through its narrative forms that constantly focus attention on presentation of the self. A whole range of psychotherapies have become common practice in U.S. society—Freudian, Jungian, eclectic, mind/body, twelve-step, and even simply confessional, to name the most familiar. Although the wide acceptance of therapy in recent decades can be seen as an antidote to the public emphasis on marketable persona, in that commonly therapy is supposed to be a search for the inner self, in other ways there are tie-ins to marketing, in that therapy often focuses on semi-public story-telling and the idea that the position and definition of the subject is in flux.

The sheer everydayness, the mundaneness, of our cultural acceptance of the different operations of personae is fascinating. We commonly understand that every social interchange, even that between only two people, involves personae. What was once the stuff of literary criticism, "persona" as the position of the author's fictional "I," has become the stuff of social interchange, in popular culture, more intimate dialogue, even courtship. Knowingly and unknowingly, we conflate different kinds of persona. We are a self-conscious lot, and memoirs are among our best-sellers.

So what's new, then, about flaunting one's persona or personae on the Web? There's been a lot of talk about blurring the lines between truth and fiction on the Web—for instance, what happens when you go into a chat room or a threaded discussion and pretend to be anybody, and engage with other personae? A lot of this talk is relatively utopian, divided between high-theory expositions about the supposedly unbounded fluidity of identity of the Web and high-tech reportage of the latest in avatar forms. My position is yet a third one, based in part on my own experience, revealing that no matter what the possibilities for identity transformation on the Web, at least in this project, a desire existed for some kind of documentary thread, some kind of representation of the integral self, some kind of communication of experience. *The Couch* gave me a unique perch from which to mull over the functions and seductions of personae on the Web.

Other art forms share an exploration of personae, particularly ones that lend themselves to narrative and portraiture. In recent photography, Laura Letinsky's subtle and allusive intimacy series of couples, as well as Wendy Ewald's ongoing involvement of children in their own self-portraiture, come to mind as compelling examples of works involving subjects and viewers in the layered ambiguities of personae. There are some qualities, though, in the representation of personae that are unique to the Web. Accordingly, I want to focus the discussion about personae and the Web on two areas: (1) the *speed* of transformation and interaction of personae, and (2) the *technological* formation of personae.

**Speed**

As I capsulized the experience for my friends, writing the character Celeste allowed me to cross myself with Mae West—Celeste had all my brazenness and none of my shyness. During most of the time I was writing the cybercharacter, I was single, dating, and in my early forties. While dating in real life was also a trying on of personae, the sheer fun of that exercise was often compromised by my own inhibitions, fears, confusions, and desires, and the inconveniently real intentions of the men I was seeing. Writing Celeste gave me a chance to try on different personae in a context that honored that kind of play, and to try different kinds of narrative voices and forms, such as the knowing-women's-mag voice, the flirtatious voice, the therapy-introspective voice, the diaristic form, the Tarot-card- reading form, and confessions about confessions. (We all wrote about what was said in the group sessions.) In the case of my character Celeste, the different voices were organized around a character trajectory, but were otherwise variable, layered, and rapidly changing. Here are a few examples of Celeste's voices:

*a.* Knowing and ironic: "Question: Do we really want men to go into therapy if what it means is that they tell us what they're feeling? Do we really want to know the convoluted things they're thinking? I always wanted to be involved with a man who's in therapy, but this idea might fall within the lines of 'be careful what you wish for, you just might get it.'"

*b.* Hedonistic: "I want to be a pleasure queen, a box of chocolates, a sand box, a whirring mind, a liquid tongue, a laughful, a handful, a mouthful."

*c.* Fortune-telling (this is from a Celeste diary many weeks later when she's falling in love): "I'm looking at the image on the Tarot card called the Tower: a medieval tower stands on top of an outcropping. Lightning hits the top, fire bursts out, a crown flies off, flames leap out the windows, and two figures fall, head first, into the air, their arms dangling over their heads."

Traditionally, what all these different narrative forms of language share is common usage in public presentation of the self. What changed with their use on the Web was their function in the unbelievable rapidity of transformation from one role to another, *dictated in large part by the speed and layering of social interchange.* While each social context is more or less a familiar one, it's the speed of the feedback loops that's unique to the Web.

I want to describe some of these layers of social interchange. The eight of us met one evening a week for a year and a half, with very few breaks—occasionally someone would take a week or two off, but there were no prolonged leaves of absence. In these meetings, we would write the group sessions together and plan character arcs and plots. In between meetings we e-mailed one another, read one another's diary entries, and wrote side episodes together, usually the adventures of two of the characters together. Sometimes we would go on the adventures and then retell them in photographs, graphics, and words for the Web. For example, my friend M. P. Dunleavey, who authored the character of Zoe, and I went to a bar in the East Village, the Horseshoe, to hang out and write a dialogue

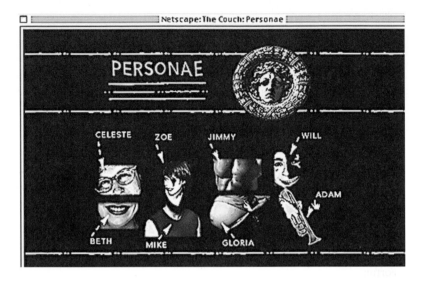

David Steuer, designer, screen grab from *The Couch,* 1997.
(**11.2**)

about our characters Celeste and Zoe hanging out and talking. We returned later with a photographer and recreated Celeste and Zoe hanging out together. It was socially very intense, almost like group therapy without the therapist, or like a lived-experience documentary project, MTV's *Real World* without the real-time camera (only occasional photo shoots) and with real friendships and acquaintanceships. Our original impetus for forming was social and to act as a kind of writing group, although the motivations for Cyborganic, our San Francisco–based server, were to explore ideas of community on the Web and to stay afloat financially at the same time. The first members of the group met at a nonprofit summer house in the Hamptons, and then again at potluck dinners in New York City sponsored by Cyborganic. Then we invited other working writers we knew to join us, forming the group of eight. We were each other's primary audience. In addition to myself, the other writers were M. P. Dunleavey, Mark Durstewitz, Christine Hull, Jay Key, Adam Penenberg, Linda Solomon, and David Steuer.

David Steuer also produced *The Couch* and designed the site. Steuer based his graphic design on blueprints for the Flatiron Building, the site

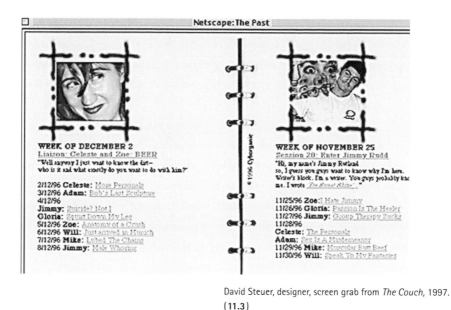

**WEEK OF DECEMBER 2**
Liaison: Celeste and Zoe: BEER
"Well anyway I just want to know the dirt—
who is it and what exactly do you want to do with him?"

2/12/96 **Celeste:** More Personals
3/12/96 **Adam:** Bob's Last Sculpture
4/12/96
**Jimmy:** Suicide? Not I
**Gloria:** Squat Down My Leg
5/12/96 **Zoe:** Anatomy of a Couch
6/12/96 **Will:** Just arrived in Munich
7/12/96 **Mike:** Label The Chains
8/12/96 **Jimmy:** Male Whoring

© 1996 Cyberspank

**WEEK OF NOVEMBER 25**
Session 20: Enter Jimmy Rudd
"Hi, my name's Jimmy Rudbud
so, I guess you guys want to know why I'm here.
Writer's block. I'm a writer. You guys probably know
me. I wrote *The Scout Slice*."

11/25/96 **Zoe:** I Hate Jimmy
11/26/96 **Gloria:** Passion Is The Healer
11/27/96 **Jimmy:** Group Therapy Sucks
11/28/96
**Celeste:** The Personals
**Adam:** Sex Is A Misdemeanor
11/29/96 **Mike:** Muscular Rum Beef
11/30/96 **Will:** Speak To My Fantasies

David Steuer, designer, screen grab from *The Couch*, 1997.
(**11.3**)

in Manhattan where the fictional sessions were supposedly being held. Employing dotted lines on a black background to suggest the plans for the foundation of the building, Steuer made an analogy between peeling back the layers of a building to its structure and the goal of therapy being to reveal the inner self (fig. 11.2). Movement within the site was similarly nested, with references leading the viewer from layer to layer—group session to diary entry, for example, or diary entry to looking at the past (fig. 11.3).

Steuer organized his "information-architecture" or site-structure design in four layers: Past, Present, Personae, and Transference. As Steuer has described his design logic, viewers could "start at the beginning and catch up, start in the present and 'flashback' to prior episodes or memories (like therapy), or select their favorite characters and allow their diary entries to be the window through which they link to the other content." Steuer illustrated each layer with color photographs or photomontages. Feedback within the group played a strong part in the evolution of the design as well as the evolution of the written text, and again it was a rapid feedback loop.

For our launch party in January 1997 at the Knitting Factory, we printed flyers on which one of the writers, Jay Key, created quotes and personae for reviewers with real names (we'd gotten in the habit of playing fast and free with public presentations of the self, and his were very funny):

"Absolutely awful, just dreadful. I know these people."—George Plimpton, editor of the *Paris Review*; "They don't sing or dance, and there is not enough sex for my taste, but I'm married to the concept."—Woody Allen, New York Knicks fan; "New York and neurosis go hand in hand. Like the Captain and Tennille. *The Couch* is where it's at, man. I don't even surf anymore. I just sit, smoke, and read."—Lou Reed, culture critic; "*The Couch* is to cyberdramas what Tennessee Williams was to the theater."—Yo Yo Ma, musician.

But then in "real life"—or at least the mass-media version of real life—we got much more press attention than we'd anticipated, starting with *The New York Times*, which sent a photographer to one of our meetings who did a double exposure of us with our alter-identities, that is to say, there were two of each of us in the image that a friend of mine described as "that high concept but utterly unreadable photograph." Still the idea of community came through in the *Times* article and photo, even if it was a community unconventionally made up of us, our readers, and our personae. The press attention fostered new roles too—we were conscious of being reviewed, a process that continued regularly for many months. Like some improv theater, we tended to go in the direction we were praised, in our case, for being "literary" on the Net—as one headline about us read, "*The New Yorker* meets *Rent* in cyberspace." We'd been thinking of ourselves more as writing group meets Web in downtown living room, so it was heady. At the same time we were doing our own public relations work, and so were conscious that to some extent our representation in the media was of our own construction too.

The public attention also fostered a competitiveness within the group that had been almost absent before. Because of the software that recorded page hits, we could trace where our readers came from and whose pages they visited on *The Couch*. For a while we shared this information every week, but we had to stop. The dynamics of the group got more performative, and these changes showed up daily on the site. We played out confrontations, attractions, and evolutions of relationships, and above all humor, which came to be the most-used social grease for both sliding from one persona to another and communicating between different characters. We tried to make each other laugh. Along with humor, the ante for shock value of confessions kept rising. Performing confessions or made-up confessions for the group became a priority. I still don't know which elements of some of the confessions were fiction or nonfiction. Sometimes I didn't want to know.

Once we launched we also performed for and were in dialogue with our readers through Transference, the interactive component. There was a group of women readers intensely interested in Celeste's dating life, who chimed in with opinions on it and about their own love lives. After awhile I found myself writing for and to them. Because of their involvement, I dwelled less on other aspects of single life, like money, and focused more on romance.

We did not get much money—just some start-up and production funds from our server Cyborganic and a little advertising—so the marketing of our characters' personae and our own personae as writers became the indirect monetary value of our work. Some print publications were fascinated by our social dynamics, such as *The New York Daily News*, for which Lynn Harris covered *The Couch* in a surprisingly lengthy three-page article.

All kinds of things happened because of this intense involvement with one another and *The Couch*. It was fun. We ate a lot of Chinese food. It was great for our writing. Friendships waxed and waned. It *was* therapeutic to some extent. It was interesting as a documentary project, in a very indirect way recording the emotions and some experiences of that year and a half. Separate from our joint writing project, it was an eventful time for life transitions: during that year and a half, two people in the group (already engaged before *The Couch* convened) married each other, another guy got engaged, I got married, one woman in her forties had her first child, two people in the group who had lived together for six years broke up, and one man grew closer to his teenage son. While most people in the group were in therapy or had been at some point, two people went into therapy for the first time.

At the same time, in our parallel universe of *The Couch*, personae transformations were rapid because our knowingness about personae collapsed. We were originally quite self-aware about narrative confessional forms, and skilled at consciously blurring the lines between fiction and nonfiction. And had we been working in a print medium, that knowledge would have held, with perhaps an additional sharpening of craft. But on the Web, where the turnaround was faster than any printed serial, we shifted so rapidly between social roles that were in turn influenced so rapidly by layers of feedback coming from different voices that writing for *The Couch* became like living in a fishbowl of improvisational theater, but one that was highly interactive with several audiences, and rewritten and represented daily. It turns out that there was a lot of pleasure in the collapse of the analytical knowledge about personae into a more performative, experiential one.

There was confusion too: a meshing of inner and outer selves, private identities and public personae. Further, we used photographs of ourselves (most other cybersoaps used posed actors for their photos), and the site was designed so viewers could easily find our real names in the bio section or e-mail us in the Transference section. So links to our "real" or established identities were always there. The design made it as easy for viewers to flip back and forth between fictional and nonfictional identities as it was for us. For the writers, in experiencing this oscillation, there evolved, oddly enough, further clarity about the distinction between performing personae and feeling deep emotions. Forms and personae shifted, but narrative and performative threads were sustained with emotions. What I mean is that our sounding board became the emotions tied to real-life experiences and threaded through the mix of performing personae. This enabled us and the viewers to stay with evolving characters and it made us better writers.

We all had very different backgrounds as writers—one woman was a staff writer at *Glamour*, another a contributing editor to *New Age Journal*, a man reported for *Forbes*, our Wunderkind producer had been director of electronic publishing in the United States for Von Holtzbrink, I'd published my Höch book with Yale University Press. In each case our writing improved, and it improved because the emotions underlying the personae formations could not change as fast as the personae themselves. The emotions had more of a documentary relationship to what was going on in our real lives than any other component of the project, even though the emotions were often indirectly expressed. So we got more adept at communicating emotion while also experimenting with different forms and changing roles. To put it colloquially, over time our masks changed more quickly in our writing and our emotions got more real. The authored emotions resonated more deeply, were more deeply felt and communicated, and they corresponded to the transitions happening in our lives.

### The Technological Creation of Personae on the Web

Although there's been a lot of talk about the presentation of personae on the Web in terms of Web content, there's been less discussion about a parallel development, technological profiling, which is gaining ever more currency. Profiling is the process of tracing a user's patterns on the Web and using that information for legal or marketing or service purposes. That profile becomes a kind of persona, although not one of the user's own conscious making. On the contrary, it is a persona that is controlled elsewhere and can even be used to manipulate the user.

Who has access to this information and how is it used? For marketing, certainly. And already for legal purposes, the electronic footprints we leave on the Web have been traced. When a California newspaper, *The Ventura County Star*, was subpoenaed in October 1997 for its records of who had visited its Web site in order to see if potential jurors had been contaminated by coverage of a murder case, it was a legal first. Defense attorneys requested unpublished e-mails and demographics of people who had participated in an online survey about the Diana Haun murder trial (she was charged with killing her lover's wife as a birthday present for him). This is a precedent, a reminder that our electronic personae, the profiles of ourselves that our computer and Web usage creates, are used in some key ways as stand-ins for ourselves. And it's not clear who will be able to control the use of these personae: privacy on the Web remains a slippery, relative concept.

I think the user needs to know who has access to the information and how it is being used, and that control should be in the user's hands. The user should be able to create and edit his or her electronic persona and see where and how and with whom it's interacting, much as we did in the seemingly separate entertainment/content world of *The Couch*. As I argued in the previous chapter, "Dirty Work and Clean Faces," graphics are our window to the information we need for that control. I see privacy issues on the Net as related to personae ones, specifically who controls the ever-evolving personae. Most users are not informed about information being collected about them on the Web; most people, including me, don't even know when "cookies" are sent—cookies are simple messages that a site sends your computer so it can recognize you the next time you visit (and often access commercial information it has stored about you)—although these are supposedly easy to trace. There is a great need for improved computer graphics that illuminate user interface with privacy guards and information-collecting agents.

In thinking more about persona issues and *The Couch*, I now see content and technological personae as two sides of the same coin—but one side that's about control and the other that's about loss of control. Issues of representation of the self link to issues of power. This comes as no surprise to those of us in cultural criticism, but often with discussions of the Web, content and technology are separated. In practice, with the creation of personae on the Web, they are not. Creation and manipulation mix on the computer screen and behind the screen.

On the Web, it's time to draw some boundaries between identity data and marketing use of that data—and the power to draw these boundaries needs to be in users' hands. I'd like to see some of *The Couch's* sense of play, of creation of dialogue, and most of all the semi-fluid evolutions of identity based on elements of the self we desired to communicate—this creative kneading of personae found in different ways in many places on the Web—injected into the building up or tearing down (depending on the user's desires) of our ever-accreting technological personae on the Web.

### Note

1. Victor Brome, *Jung: Man and Myth* (New York: Atheneum, 1981), 276.

# Credits

*Clean New World* was funded in part by a grant from the National Endowment for the Arts.

Most of the writings in this book appeared in other forms in the following magazines and museum catalogs which have kindly given their permission to reprint them. Each of the essays has been revised for this volume.

**I: Modernism**

2. "Heartfield in Context," *Art in America* (Feb. 1985).

3. "The Circle of New Advertising Designers," in *Montage and Modern Life 1919– 1942*, ed. Matthew Teitelbaum (Cambridge: MIT Press, 1992).

4. "ringl + pit: The Representation of Women in German Advertising, 1929–33," *The Print Collector's Newsletter* (July–Aug. 1985).

**II: Post-WWII and Today**

5. "Design in the Service of Commerce," in *Graphic Design in America*, ed. Mildred Friedman (New York: Harry N. Abrams, 1989).

6. "New Traditionalism and Corporate Identity," *Artforum* (Oct. 1989).

7. "Collectivism in the Decade of Greed, Political Art Coalitions in the 1980s in New York City," in *Public Domain*, ed. Jorge Ribalta (Barcelona: Centre de Santa Monica, 1994).

8. "Portfolio: Women and Design" uses some excerpts from "The Fashionable Barbara Kruger," *Harper's Bazaar* (Feb. 1994); "Watching W.A.C.," *I.D. Magazine* (Nov./Dec. 1992); "Sylvia Harris Woodard," *I.D. Magazine* (Jan. 1996).

9. "A Baby and a Coathanger: TV-News and Other Graphics on Abortion," in *TV News Aesthetic*, ed. Lawrence Mirsky (New York: Princeton Architectural Press and Cooper Union, 1995).

**III: The Internet**

10. "Dirty Work and Clean Faces: The Look of Intelligent Agents on the Internet," *Print* (March/April 1996).

11. "Confessions from *The Couch*: Issues of Persona on the Web," *Afterimage* (July–Aug. 1998).

# Index

Index compiled by Celeste Newbrough.

**Note to Index**

Titles of organizations or journals are listed in lower case when needed to replicate the authentic spelling. Figures are listed as page numbers. The figure number is given only when needed to further identify the figure. The following abbreviations are used in the index:

f = figure

n = note

**Index**